Torture and the Ticking Bomb

Blackwell Public Philosophy
Edited by Michael Boylan, Marymount University

In a world of 24-hour news cycles and increasingly specialized knowledge, the Blackwell Public Philosophy series takes seriously the idea that there is a need and demand for engaging and thoughtful discussion of topics of broad public importance. Philosophy itself is historically grounded in the public square, bringing people together to try to understand the various issues that shape their lives and give them meaning. This 'love of wisdom' – the essence of philosophy – lies at the heart of the series. Written in an accessible, jargon-free manner by internationally renowned authors, each book is an invitation to the world beyond news flashes and sound bites and into public wisdom.

Permission to Steal: Revealing the Roots of Corporate Scandal by Lisa H. Newton
The Extinction of Desire: A Tale of Enlightenment by Michael Boylan
Doubting Darwin? Creationist Designs on Evolution by Sahotra Sarkar
Torture and the Ticking Bomb by Bob Brecher

Forthcoming
Terrorism and Counter-Terrorism: An Applied Philosophical Approach by Seumas Miller
Spiritual But Not Religious: The Evolving Science of the Soul by Christian Erickson
In Defence of Dolphins: The New Moral Frontier by Thomas I. White
Evil On-Line: Explorations of Evil and Wickedness on the Web by Dean Cocking and Jeroen van den Hoven

For further information about individual titles in the series, supplementary material, and regular updates, visit www.blackwellpublishing.com/publicphilosophy

Torture and
the Ticking Bomb

Bob Brecher

Blackwell
Publishing

© 2007 by Bob Brecher

BLACKWELL PUBLISHING
350 Main Street, Malden, MA 02148–5020, USA
9600 Garsington Road, Oxford OX4 2DQ, UK
550 Swanston Street, Carlton, Victoria 3053, Australia

The right of Bob Brecher to be identified as the Author of this Work has been
asserted in accordance with the UK Copyright, Designs, and Patents Act 1988.

First published 2007 by Blackwell Publishing Ltd

1   2007

Library of Congress Cataloging-in-Publication Data

Brecher, Robert.
    Torture and the ticking bomb / Bob Brecher.
       p. cm.
    Includes bibliographical references and index.
    ISBN 978-1-4051-6201-2 (hardback : alk. paper) – ISBN 978-1-4051-6202-9 (pbk. :
alk. paper)   1. Torture.   2. Human rights.   I. Title.

    HV8593.B74 2007
    363.2′32–dc22

                                                                        2006103174

A catalogue record for this title is available from the British Library.

Set in 11 on 13 pt Minion
by SNP Best-set Typesetter Ltd, Hong Kong
Printed and bound in Singapore
by Utopia Press Pte Ltd

The publisher's policy is to use permanent paper from mills that operate a sustain-
able forestry policy, and which has been manufactured from pulp processed using
acid-free and elementary chlorine-free practices. Furthermore, the publisher
ensures that the text paper and cover board used have met acceptable environmen-
tal accreditation standards.

For further information on
Blackwell Publishing, visit our website:
www.blackwellpublishing.com

In memory of my parents,
Božena Brecherová and Helmut Brecher,
and of my friend, Graham Burton Laker.

Contents

Preface

We live in times when, as Conor Gearty has pointed out, 'legal scholars in the US are being taken seriously when they float the idea of torture warrants as a reform to what they see as the unacceptably uncodified system of arbitrary torture that they believe currently prevails'. And he is right when he goes on to add that 'This is like reacting to a series of police killings with proposals to reform the law on homicide so as to sanction officially approved pre-trial executions'. [1]

It is because the general public is taking these academics seriously that there is an urgent need to expose how spurious their ideologically driven arguments are. The "respectability" they confer on the argument that so-called ticking bombs justify torture, and that it had therefore better be regulated, needs to be countered. Otherwise there is a real danger that western politicians will succeed in persuading us to go along with them when they insist that another basic freedom – freedom from torture – is yet one more value we must abandon in the endless "war on terrorism". It is a short road from legalizing torture intended to gain information to accepting torture as a legitimate weapon and for all sorts of purposes. The "intellectual respectability" conferred by the academy is essential for that enterprise. Thus, since Alan Dershowitz's carefully constructed proposal to introduce torture warrants is both the most prominent and the most sophisticated of today's attempts to make torture respectable, it is his proposal we need to focus on.

In the Introduction, I say something about both the intellectual and the political contexts of the so-called ticking bomb scenario that is the basis of these proposals. In chapter two I argue that the "ticking bomb" scenario remains in crucial respects a fantasy; and that the grounds it is said to offer for justifying interrogational torture so as to avoid a putative catastrophe are spurious. In chapter three I argue that, whatever you think of those arguments, the consequences of legalizing interrogational torture, and thus institutionalizing it, would be so disastrous as to outweigh any such catastrophes anyway. Finally, in chapter four, I draw together what the details of my argument imply about torture in general and interrogational torture in particular; and about why any even semi-decent society must abhor torture – in all circumstances, always, everywhere.

Writing this book has not been easy, and I owe a great deal to everyone who has supported me over the last eighteen months, both friends and colleagues, as well as to all those, too many to name, from whose conversation I have benefitted. I want in particular to thank Gideon Calder, Mark Devenney, Angela Fenwick, Jo Halliday, Richard Jackson, Carol Jones, Alyce von Rothkirch, Doris Schroeder, Phil Vellender and Sophie Whiting for their comments on sections of the manuscript and for their encouragement; audiences at conferences on the Barbarisation of Warfare at the University of Wolverhampton in June 2005 and on The Concept of War: Political Science, Philosophy, Law in Vancouver in September 2006, as well as their organizers; and to those who took part in Philosophy Society meetings at the Universities of Brighton and Newport. Finally, my thanks to an anonymous reviewer for their helpful comments on the final draft; to colleagues at Blackwell Publishing with whom it has been a pleasure to work – Nick Bellorini, the model of a professional editor, Gillian Kane, Brigitte Lee, Kelvin Matthews, Jack Messenger and indexer Marie Lorimer; and to Michael Boylan, the editor of a series with which I am proud to be associated.

Any profits from this book will be shared with Amnesty UK and the Medical Foundation for the Care of Victims of Torture.

Bob Brecher
Brighton

Chapter One

Introduction

Suppose there is good reason to think that someone has planted a bomb in a public place. And suppose there is good reason to think that it is going to go off in the next two hours or so, and that it is going to kill and maim dozens of people, maybe hundreds. The question is all too real. Imagine, to bring the example closer to home, that the police or the secret services had known that bombs were shortly to go off *somewhere* in Bali, Madrid, London or Sharm-el-Sheikh in the attacks of 2004 and 2005. But no one knows where the bomb is – except one person, who is already in custody. Naturally they have no intention of revealing where the bomb is. Maybe they have planted it themselves; maybe not. Either way, they remain silent. Should they be tortured to force them to reveal where the bomb is?

Or take an example of the ticking bomb scenario from an actual policy blueprint, hyperbolic though it is:

al-Qaeda has other *sleeper cells* within the United States that may be planning similar attacks [to 11 September 2001]. Indeed, al-Qaeda plans apparently include efforts to develop and *deploy chemical, biological and nuclear weapons of mass destruction*. Under these circumstances, a detainee may possess information that could enable the United States to prevent *attacks that potentially could equal or surpass the September 11 attacks in their magnitude*. Clearly, any harm that might occur during an interrogation would pale to insignificance compared to the harm avoided by preventing such an attack, which could take *hundreds or thousands of lives*. [1]

Until recently I would have argued that 'Whatever one might have to say about torture, there appear to be moral reasons for not saying it'. [2] Even to raise the issue, I would probably have thought, is to give publicity to what is so abhorrent as to be beyond discussion. It remains a position I respect. Slavoj Žižek, for instance, insists that 'essays . . . which do not advocate torture outright, [but] simply introduce it as a legitimate topic of debate, are even more dangerous than an explicit endorsement of torture'. [3] But in the end, present reality demands a direct response, despite that danger.

Two things in particular have changed my mind. First, the revelations from Abu Ghraib, Guantanamo Bay and elsewhere are a gruesome reminder that, at the beginning of the twenty-first century and official policy notwithstanding, torture remains a weapon in the armoury of "civilized" states. Jennifer Harbury's exposé of longstanding American collusion in torture is testament enough to that. [4] The hypocrisy of official policy was underscored by growing evidence of the widespread practice of outsourcing the torture of prisoners to countries such as Egypt, Jordan, Morocco and Singapore. "Rendition", as American newspeak has it, appears to have become standard practice – and one in which European states collude. [5] We have come a very long way in the twenty-five years since Henry Shue, a longstanding campaigner against torture, felt he had to justify raising the issue at all. Second, it has become clear that the United States government's underwriting of torture since the attacks of 11 September 2001, as a means of conducting its so-called war on terror, has not come out of the blue. It has emerged against a background of academics, largely lawyers, seriously advocating that torture be legally permitted under certain circumstances. The normalizing discourse provided by legal advocates of interrogational torture is an important source of legitimation for a policy of encouraging such torture, and of what follows in its wake: 'the hypothetical has wedged us into the position of admitting that torture is sometimes a legitimate tactic', as a recent writer comments. [6]

That was something new; and something very serious. Of course, torture had been ubiquitous in the second half of the twentieth century, from the Nazis Europe-wide to the French in Algeria, the British in Malaya, Kenya and Northern Ireland, the Americans in Vietnam, the Israelis in the Occupied Territories and dozens of regimes in their own countries. Nonetheless, until very recently there has been more or less unanimous agreement that torture was always wrong, whenever, wherever and for whatever reason it was carried out. Or at least, so it appears. For that agreement, admittedly widespread, was only a qualified agreement: it turns out that almost every writer since the early 1970s who discusses, and as a matter of course condemns, torture nonetheless thinks that it *is* justifiable in the extreme case, even if in no other (and whatever their view of the realism of such cases).

My initial anger remains, that we should have reached a point where it has become necessary to revisit what for 200 years was rightly taken for granted, namely that torture is quite simply wrong, always, everywhere. But that anger requires that I take seriously what Dershowitz and others are saying. How else to refute the arguments than by questioning their often barely argued premises and exploring the likely consequences? As I started, I also found myself increasingly annoyed that – doubtless inadvertently – careless philosophizing about imaginary ticking bomb scenarios had given their argument a starting-point which should never have been conceded. For it is on the basis of unwarranted assumptions about such scenarios that academics are now explicitly advocating interrogational torture, its legalization, or both. To put it bluntly: when a couple of academics can seriously argue that 'torture is "morally defensible" even if it causes the deaths of innocent people', and seek American publication for their paper 'because Americans were "more open to new ideas on human rights"', [7] then it is time to get one's intellectual hands dirty. Richard Jackson is right: 'There is no starker illustration of western society's current moral vacuity than the serious public debate about torturing terrorist suspects – not to mention its all-too-common practice by America and its allies'. [8] Challenging that vacuity demands that we confront what feeds it.

What is Torture?

Should we try to define torture? No: we should not be looking for a definition. That is not because the idea of torture is in some way particularly recalcitrant. Rather, it is because it is impossible to define real things, such as tables, rivers, kindness or unhappiness, since, as part of the real world, they can change without becoming something else. For instance, you cannot define this particular book. You cannot specify exactly what makes it the book it is: it remains the book it is even if you tear out a couple of pages or add some notes. Real things, like this book, or like torture, can be only described; they cannot be specified exactly, that is to say, defined. It is only our own inventions, our ideas – or at least some of them – which can be defined, or specified exactly: a metre, a triangle, legal guilt, a metaphor. [9] Unlike with real things, if you take anything away from one of these, or add anything to it, it would be something different. It is in part the widespread assumption that torture needs to be unambiguously defined before we can say anything about it that enables American – and other – governments to get away with trying 'to avoid admitting to apparent cases of torture by simply denying that they qualify as torture at all': [10]

> The White House Counsel said that President Bush 'has given no order or directive that would immunize from prosecution anyone engaged in conduct that constitutes torture. All interrogation techniques actually authorized have been carefully vetted, are lawful, and do not constitute torture'. [11]

But would not a clear definition of torture help rule it out? Again, no. Trying to define torture is not only mistaken, it is counter-productive. Consider the infamous Bybee memorandum, for example, which allows those who advocate the use of torture under other names to manipulate definitions so as to pretend to themselves, and to persuade others, that torture is not torture. Thus Bybee would have it that inflicting severe pain does not amount to torture unless it attains a 'level that would ordinarily be associated with a sufficiently serious physical condition or injury such as death, organ failure, or serious impairment of body functions'; [12] while 'Porter Goss, the CIA director, defended waterboarding [repeated near-drowning] in March 2005 testimony before the Senate as a "professional interrogation technique"'. [13] By definition, then, anything just short of that is not torture – and thus not ruled out, whether legally or morally. Thus, while torture by the American occupying forces in Iraq is rife, those responsible are able to hide behind the fact that 'harsh interrogation' [14] appears definitionally not to be torture. And it is all too easy to think that 'harsh interrogation' is not torture because, as with white noise or drugs some decades ago, it does not fall within a particular definition of torture.

The United Nations' own Convention Against Torture (1984) is problematic in just this way. It defines torture as the intentional infliction of 'severe pain or suffering, whether physical or mental . . . by or at the instigation or with the consent or acquiescence of a public official or other person acting in an official capacity', and explicitly excludes any 'pain or suffering arising only from, inherent in or incidental to lawful sanction'. [15] Under this definition, if interrogational torture were made legal – if torture warrants were made a lawful sanction in certain cases of withholding information – then it would no longer count as torture, since it was 'inherent in . . . lawful sanction'! [16]

Torture cannot and need not be defined. It is not that "I know it when I see it" (although I might); but that, just as in debates about pornography and abortion, there are bound to be borderline cases, and these borderlines are bound to change over time, as new technology is developed. The point is that there are cases which indubitably count, even if there are others which remain unclear or undecidable. Images of young children being sodomized by an adult or an animal, for example, *obviously* constitute pornography. A newborn child is *clearly* not a foetus, even if the borderline between foetus and child remains controversial. It is attention to actual practice that removes the temptation to define: an Abu Ghraib guard accused of torture could not sincerely claim that 'I am shocked – shocked! – to find that "waterboarding" or squeezing prisoners' genitals or setting dogs on them is regarded as torture'. [17] What I propose, therefore, is a description of torture, taken from Christopher Tindale (though he himself regards it as a definition) and based on the United Nations General Assembly's Convention Against Torture (1984):

> any act by which severe pain or suffering, whether physical or mental, is intentionally inflicted on a person for such purposes as obtaining from that person or a third person information or confession, punishing that person for an act committed or suspected to have been committed, or intimidating or dehumanizing that person or other persons. [18]

That seems to me adequately to describe torture. Any act like that is *sufficient* to count as torture. By contrast, what is *necessary* for an act to count as torture is liable to change. Once invented, waterboarding is always enough to constitute an act of torture. New methods, however, are also always liable to be invented, so that what is needed for an act to constitute torture cannot be specified in advance.

Dershowitz on Interrogational Torture

Let me now focus on the proposal to legalize interrogational torture. Its leading advocate is Alan Dershowitz, a civil rights lawyer of some thirty years' standing. Initially presented in various American newspapers and on a number of websites, and then brought together in chapter 4 of *Why Terrorism Works*, [19] his arguments are the most prominent. Certainly, his advocacy of the legal institutionalization of torture in cases 'When torture is the least evil of terrible options' [20] is the most notorious and most comprehensive elaboration of what is often called the "new realism" about torture. He is not alone in his "realism", as we shall see – although hardly anyone else wants to see torture legalized. His arguments are far more sophisticated than those directly advocating interrogational torture, however, as well as being the most influential, and thus the most dangerous. I shall therefore focus closely on Dershowitz's work.

What, then, is his basic argument? Derived intellectually from Jeremy Bentham, [21] it has two parts. First, there are some extraordinary cases where interrogational torture is, or is regarded as, the least bad option, namely variants of the ticking bomb scenario. (As we shall see in chapter three, his own understanding of which of these two very different positions his argument rests on is at variance from most of his critics' understanding of the matter.) Second, since torture is *de facto* used in these cases, it is better to drop the hypocritical pretence that it is something "we" don't do and legalize its use. It would be better to issue 'non-lethal torture warrants in extraordinary cases', [22] he argues, than to go along with the hypocrisy of torture's 'selective use beneath the radar screen'. [23] He has two main reasons. First, legal regulation would as a matter of fact reduce instances of torture and restrict its use to the minimum necessary to obtain the required information. Second, honesty is always the best policy, here as elsewhere.

Dershowitz's proposal is rooted historically in his role in recent Israeli debates, and specifically those around the Landau Commission's 1987 effective legitimatization of torture [24] – when 'the use of torture to prevent terrorism' in Israel 'was very real and recurring' [25] – and the subsequent High Court's outlawing of it in 1999. Dershowitz's initial public intervention, in 1989, was to question the hypocrisy of the Landau Commission's sanctioning 'physical pressure' but not calling it torture. [26] Unsurprisingly, the 1999 judgement refers to his paper (in section 34). More significant, however, is the fact that 'the High Court added, in section 37 of the decision, that "if the State wishes to enable GSS [General Security Service] investigators to utilize physical means in interrogations, they must seek the enactment of legislation for this purpose".... It seemed, to some, that, quite perversely, the court ended its own deliberations on torture by somehow winking to the Knesset [Israeli Parliament] to decide on this issue'. [27] It was in 2001 that Dershowitz started very publicly to advocate torture warrants. [28] His recent proposal that in certain circumstances preemptive strikes should also be legalized perhaps illuminates his overall agenda:

> while it may well be necessary for democracies to fight terrorists with one hand tied behind their backs, it is neither necessary nor desirable for a democracy to fight with two hands tied behind its back, especially when the ropes that bind the second hand are anachronistic laws that can be changed without compromising legitimate human rights. [29]

Let me take another example to make his position clearer. Most advocates of legalizing the consumption of, say, cannabis, think that, because taking cannabis is morally unproblematic, it should be made legal. Others, however, think that taking cannabis should be legalized despite its being morally wrong, because the consequences of prohibition are worse than what they think the consequences would be of legalization: in particular, the benefits of regulation would be greater control of the quality of cannabis consumed, and – perhaps – a diminution of the amount consumed. And so with interrogational torture. Some think torture in the ticking bomb case is morally justified, and therefore should be legalized, on pain of hypocrisy and in order to guarantee that torture be used only in tightly specified cases. Dershowitz thinks, whether or not consistently, that although such torture is morally wrong, it should nevertheless be legalized, again on pain of hypocrisy and to control and regulate the practice. Almost all opponents of either of those positions argue that, while at the extreme torture is indeed morally justified, it should remain illegal precisely because of the likely consequences of legalization, which they think, far from limiting torture, would be the thin end of an unwelcome wedge.

Why Write about Torture?

My primary reason for writing this book is simply that too many people seem to think that torture is justifiable in the ticking bomb case. Surely, if it is a question of the non-lethal torture of one person against hundreds or thousands of people being blown up, then if they have to be tortured to get the information which would prevent the catastrophe, then that is that. So maybe it is not surprising that when Dershowitz asked American audiences 'for a show of hands' in the wake of the 2001 attacks on the twin towers and the Pentagon, they should have voted nearly unanimously in favour of torturing a "terrorist suspect" in such circumstances. [30] But it is by no means just the American public who agree with Dershowitz:

> When the B'Tselem [an Israeli human rights organization] reports [on torture as practised by the Israeli GSS] came out, and were presented in press conferences in Israel and around the world, workers in B'Tselem were prepared for all kinds of responses: denial, disbelief, shock. But we were the ones who were shocked, for the one consistent response (even from people abroad) was that torture was a necessary evil. [31]

In the aftermath of the London bombings of 7 July 2005, the mindset which invokes 'necessary evil' has taken considerable hold in the UK, especially among its politicians and in large sections of the media. Detention without trial of foreign nationals suspected of terrorism and the extra-judicial execution of Jean Charles de Menezes, an entirely innocent electrician, to take just two examples, were enthusiastically supported in sections of the media, and sometimes met with relief, even triumphalism, rather than being condemned. [32]

As I have said, the thought, however reluctant, of nearly all Dershowitz's critics is that there are cases where torturing a person to gain the information that only they have and that is needed to prevent the deaths of thousands of innocent people is indeed justifiable. But it is a thought too far: the ticking bomb scenario is sheer fantasy. As

I shall argue in detail in the following chapter, when carefully thought through, many of the various different conditions that Dershowitz and others assume to hold in such scenarios are themselves at best wildly implausible. And when they are put together to form the requisite "scenario", the construction falls apart. The concession most of Dershowitz's critics make, therefore – that the ticking bomb case he proposes represents a real problem – is both unnecessary and counter-productive.

The problem is that the ticking bomb fantasy derives from philosophers' thought-experiments, which are usually designed to test the limits of moral theory. In the most extreme case, it is commonly claimed, the beneficial consequences of an action *must* outweigh what is repugnant about it. I have no doubt that the question of whether or not the beneficial consequences of an action might in principle morally outweigh what is morally repugnant about it is an extremely important and interesting theoretical issue in moral philosophy; and that thought-experiments can be helpful in trying to think about it. But to use a hypothetical example as though it were a real case without first considering very carefully its plausibility in the real world is intellectually and politically irresponsible. I shall return to this issue at the end of the book. Here, I want just to emphasize that a statement such as Martha Nussbaum's, that I 'don't think any sensible moral position would deny that there might be some imaginable situations in which torture [of a particular individual] is justified' [33] simply *assumes* that moral absolutism cannot be a 'sensible moral position' to take here. It is such careless pronouncements which have helped create a climate in which a senior American judge can pronounce that 'if the stakes are high enough torture is permissible. No one who doubts that should be in a position of responsibility'; [34] and where an academic lawyer can breezily announce that 'we [meaning only himself, of course] cannot completely reject the evil of torture as a method of combating terrorism, regardless of what international law provides'. [35] At least some of the actual practitioners of torture are rather blunter: 'If you don't violate someone's human rights some of the time, you probably aren't doing your job'. [36]

However, there is a more immediate and more important reason for focusing on *interrogational* torture. Unless there is something seriously wrong with you, I take it that you find torture morally abhorrent. I mean torture, the point of which is something other than to obtain life-saving information: torture as a means of revenge, intimidation, punishment or dehumanization. All over the world, as organizations such as Amnesty International and Human Rights Watch repeatedly testify, people are being tortured in pursuit of these ends, in all probability even as you read these words. And not only that. People are all too often tortured for the sadistic pleasure of it. Whatever your convictions about what sorts of punishment particular crimes merit, or what degree of intimidation might be reasonable in what circumstances or even when, if ever, revenge is justified, you surely cannot countenance torture in any of these cases – let alone in order to gratify the torturer or the onlooker. Can you?

Still, even if I am not being over-optimistic on that score you might think that there are *some* cases where torture is justified. That is to say, you might think that if there are any circumstances at all where torture might be justifiable, then it is in the circumstances of the ticking bomb scenario; if any form of torture, for any reason at all, is justifiable, then it is justifiable where it is the only possible means of getting the information needed to prevent the death and maiming of hundreds of innocent people. Nothing else could even conceivably justify torturing anyone. But *that* does. Saving all those lives outweighs even torture. In the words of a professional torturer: 'It is necessary to get the information now because from now on to the future it might be too late. And to save time, everything is valid.' [37]

You might even think that, because the person concerned is not innocent (they know where the bomb is), torturing them in order to obtain vital information is even more different from other sorts of torture. They have the information, and are therefore already guilty. Furthermore, and precisely because of that, the torturer's power over them is limited. If they tell the interrogators right away where the bomb is, there will be no torture; if they delay, the torture will end as soon as they confess. In short, it is *their fault* they are being tortured. But this reasoning is appalling, as Tindale reminds us. When jurors were asked how they could have acquitted the police concerned when they had seen the video of their beating Rodney King in the infamous case of 1991–2, one 'told Reuters that it was a matter of interpreting the video. Looked at carefully, it showed that King was in control of his situation', since 'once King complied and allowed himself to be handcuffed, then the beatings stopped. Hence at any point in the procedures King could have ended the beating simply by complying with police requests'. [38] Or consider Seamus Miller's bizarre argument that 'the terrorist is forcing the police to choose between two evils, namely torturing the terrorist or allowing thousands of lives to be lost', because in refusing to say where the bomb is, 'the terrorist is preventing the police from preventing him from completing his (joint) action of murdering thousands of innocent people'. [39] In shifting responsibility onto the person under torture in those circumstances, Miller's position would allow blame for how anyone deemed guilty was treated to shift from those actually treating them in that way to the allegedly guilty party. 'She made me do it!' the woman's husband could legitimately say to anyone objecting to his assaulting her: by refusing to reveal her lover's name, she was preventing him from preventing her from doing something wrong. *And* he had warned her what would happen if she were ever "unfaithful".

To put the central point a little more formally: interrogational torture constitutes the limiting case of objections to torture. If even interrogational torture is morally unjustifiable, then so is every other sort of torture. So if I can show that even interrogational torture in the most extreme circumstances remains unjustifiable, then I will have made a case against all forms of torture, against torture as an instrument of revenge, intimidation, punishment, humiliation or sadistic expression.

The Agenda

My main aim in this book, therefore, is to persuade you that the increasingly modish "realism" which would permit interrogational torture – it's going to happen anyway, so we had better come to terms with it – is fundamentally misconceived. And since this "realism" is based on the so-called ticking bomb scenario, that is my immediate target. If I succeed, then I will not only have undermined the basis of all too much state practice – a practice I would describe as constituting state terrorism – but at the same time I would also have taken away the first rung of the ladder of realpolitik which in the actually existing world leads inexorably from interrogational to other forms of torture. My two targets are thus interrogational torture itself and the proposal to legalize it in certain circumstances, rather than torture in general. That would require quite another book (although I do say something at the end about where I think a comprehensive argument against torture might start).

My first move is to show that the "new realism" is in fact based in fantasy: no argument based on a ticking bomb scenario should even get off the ground. The second, and the more complicated one, is to argue that both advocates of legalizing interrogational torture, such as Dershowitz, and those who would allow it in retrospect, albeit without legalizing the practice, pay far too little attention to the practical issues of interrogational torture in such supposed cases; and in the case of the former, to the broader issues that would arise were interrogational torture to be legalized. In short, their case is poorly argued; it makes remarkably little reference to relevant counter-evidence; and, far from being "realistic", it takes extraordinary little account of reality.

One more point before turning to the argument itself: the question of the utilitarianism in which Dershowitz's and others' "modest proposals" are based. All those who advocate interrogational torture, whether legalized or not, simply assume some variety of a utilitarian understanding of morality: if the benefit of an action outweighs its disbenefits, then that action is morally justified. I am convinced that is wrong; but I also think that this is not the place to make *that* argument. For my concern here is not with moral theory, but with practical morality and the real world of politics. I want to counter the popular appeal that the argument for legalization actually has. And it is one or other form of utilitarianism – the basic view that what makes an action right or wrong is its consequences, in terms of net benefit or disbenefit (interpreted differently by different sorts of utilitarians) – which broadly underpins not only everyday politics, but also the moral perspective of perhaps the majority of people. That is why I shall restrict myself to utilitarian considerations, despite my own conviction that the theory offers a wholly inadequate understanding of morality. Because it is utilitarianism which is so often at the root of public policy, I think that what is centrally important is to show that arguments advocating interrogational torture in the ticking bomb scenario and/or its legalization are spurious even on their own utilitarian terms. Regarding torture, 'we must weigh what we might gain against what we might lose, and we always lose too much'. [40]

Not everyone is a utilitarian, of course. Some people think that (broadly Kantian) considerations about not treating people merely as a means to an end, but always also as an end in themselves – that everyone demands and deserves unqualified respect simply as rational beings – are enough to show that torture is always wrong. For what could be more humiliating, what greater form of disrespect could there be, than torturing a person, than breaking who they are and to that extent making them not a person at all (see chapter four)? What clearer example than torture could there be of treating a person merely as a means to an end? That is why torture is *absolutely* forbidden by international human rights law: there are no exceptions. Others, however, think that it is pretty obvious that the ticking bomb scenario shows just what is wrong with this sort of view. A moral theory which permits the death and maiming of hundreds, maybe thousands, of people rather than torturing one person who has the information to prevent such carnage simply exposes its own absurdity. (Doubtless they would point to Kant's own example of turning over an innocent person to their pursuers in the knowledge that they will be killed rather than lying about the person's whereabouts.) The point is that it will not do 'to play the student in Philosophy 101', as Sanford Levinson puts it, 'where Kantian deontologists contend with utilitarians as to the propriety of lying to Nazis or killing a single innocent in order to save the world. (For) unless one *is* a Kantian, it is hard to understand why one would embrace this position'. [41] Maybe so; maybe not. My own view is that the Kantian position is broadly right. Certainly, there is more than one way of saying what is wrong with torture. What matters here, however, is that it be said; and that I address those who are *not* already convinced that Kant is enough to dispose of interrogational torture.

So I shall put issues of moral theory to one side. My purpose is directly to counter contemporary arguments for the moral legitimacy and/or the legalization of, specifically, interrogational torture. Since those are utilitarian, I shall not quarrel with that theory here. Only right at the end shall I briefly come back to it.

Chapter Two

The Fantasy of the Ticking Bomb Scenario

Dershowitz's Argument and the Ticking Bomb

Dershowitz's elaboration of the ticking bomb scenario represents by far the most sophisticated advocacy of legalizing interrogational torture (and, as I have said, in the view of some, though not himself, of interrogational torture itself). He begins by telling us how he has

> always challenged (my) students with hypothetical and real-life problems requiring them to choose among evils. . . . The classic hypothetical case involves the train engineer whose brakes become inoperative. There is no way he can stop his speeding vehicle of death. Either he can do nothing, in which case he will plow into a busload of schoolchildren, or he can swerve onto another track, where he sees a drunk lying on the rails. (Neither decision will endanger him or his passengers.) There is no third choice. What should he do? [1]

Drawing on this version of the classic "trolley problem", [2] he reminds us that we are sometimes faced with an unavoidable moral dilemma which demands that we choose the lesser of two evils. We have to choose: the only question is what should guide that choice. Should it be the number of people involved; who those people are; both of these; or what? Even leaving it to chance is a decision. However you decide, *someone* is going to suffer the consequences. In these circumstances, unless you really do think that the consequences of what you do is not morally to the point, you are likely to choose that course of action which leads to the least suffering possible in the circumstances –

however you conceptualize that suffering and whatever account you take of issues such as the identity of those suffering, the length of their suffering or the length and/or quality of their lives so far. The problem is all too familiar, especially for health workers and for those caught up in all sorts of violence. Nor will less than complete certainty of success save us from having to face such a dilemma. The attempted 'swerve' might fail, but still, the train driver has to try. And so with torture to prevent catastrophe: 'It is impossible to avoid the difficult moral dilemma of choosing among evils by denying the empirical reality that torture *sometimes* works, even if it does not always work. No technique of crime prevention always works.' [3]

Dershowitz goes on to point out that in Israel in the 1980s and 1990s,

> the use of torture to prevent terrorism was not hypothetical; it was very real and recurring. I soon discovered that virtually no one was willing to take the "purist" position against torture in the ticking bomb case . . .

and concludes that if

> the reason you permit nonlethal torture is based on the ticking bomb case, why not limit it exclusively to that compelling but rare situation? Moreover, if you believe that nonlethal torture is justifiable in the ticking bomb case, why not require advance judicial approval – a 'torture warrant'? [4]

Briefly to remind ourselves, the substantial position is this. First, there are some extraordinary cases where interrogational torture is the least bad option, namely variants of the ticking bomb scenario. Second, since torture is going to remain present in the real world anyway, it is better to drop the hypocritical pretence that it is something "we" don't do and legalize the use of interrogational torture in relevant cases. The argument seems disarmingly simple: sometimes it is necessary to do what is least bad, and we cannot wish away that reality. Better, surely, that – if absolutely necessary – one person be tortured than that hundreds or thousands be killed and maimed. And since such circumstances are inevitably going to arise, it is better that torture be legally regulated, so as both to avoid abuse and to ensure that it is used as sparingly as possible.

But the appearance of simplicity is deceptive. When we look closely at the scenario on which it is based, it turns out that it really is just a fantasy – and not merely in the sense simply of being unrealistic or far-fetched. It is a fantasy because its conditions run counter to each other. The circumstances of the purported scenario preclude just the "solution" proposed – the legalization of interrogational torture in those cases in which the competent authority issues the requisite warrant. It is central for the argument that there be sufficient urgency to justify torture – but not so much that there is not enough time for the judge(s) (or whoever) to consider whether or not the case merits a warrant to torture; that the torture be effective enough to elicit the information needed in the short time available; that the information the captive gives under torture will be accurate rather than designed to mislead in order to buy time; and of course that they actually have the information in the first place (and although Dershowitz equivocates somewhat about how many "mistakes" are tolerable, unlike others he at least recognizes the issue). Military, political and legal apologists for torture often combine these conditions under the single notion of necessity: torture is necessary to avoid catastrophe. When it is unpacked, however, the argument falls apart. The time and effectiveness conditions run against each other; the likelihood of accurate information is very far from certain; and the necessity which the circumstances press upon the authorities can only ever be retrospective: we cannot know in advance that we are faced with such a case. As Michael Davis nicely puts it, 'Realists pay surprisingly little attention to reality'. [5] Before going into these and other details, however, I want to discuss the ticking bomb scenario itself, since its uncritical acceptance in the first place helps obscure them.

Dershowitz is of course right that the 'scenario has been discussed by many philosophers' and that the consensus 'across the political spectrum from civil libertarians to law-and-order advocates' [6] is that in such a case torture is permissible. The ticking bomb scenario is indeed the touchstone of discussions of torture. Here is how Corey Robin's review of Sanford Levinson's recent collection of essays on the subject opens:

If *Torture* is any indication of contemporary sensibilities, neo-cons in the White House are not the only ones in thrall to romantic notions of danger and catastrophe. Academics are too. Every scholarly discussion of torture, and the essays collected in *Torture* are no exception, begins with the ticking time bomb scenario. . . . What to do?

It's an interesting question. But given that it is so often posed in the name of moral realism, we might consider a few facts before we rush to answer it. [7]

Indeed we might. Consider the scenario presented by Jean Bethke Elshtain in her contribution to the book:

A bomb has been planted in an elementary school building. There are several such buildings in the city in question. A known member of a terrorist criminal gang has been apprehended. The authorities are as close to 100 percent certain as human beings can be in such circumstances that the man apprehended has specific knowledge of which school contains the deadly bomb, due to go off within the hour. He refuses to divulge the information as to which school, and officials know they cannot evacuate all of the schools, thereby guaranteeing the safety of thousands of school children. It follows that some four hundred children will soon die unless the bomb is disarmed. Are you permitted to torture a suspect in order to gain the information that might spare the lives of so many innocents? [8]

While opposing warrants, Elshtain nonetheless thinks interrogational torture is morally justifiable. As Robin eloquently puts it, it 'is not the routinizing of *torture*' that she objects to; 'it is the *routinizing* of torture' [9] that she thinks wrong.

Her "example", however, is strikingly careless. The bomb is 'due to go off within the hour': so why can't 'officials' simply pick up the phone to every school in the city? Why on earth can't they 'evacuate all of the schools'? What even remotely plausible "facts" would have to be filled in to answer that question? This is not just a fantasy; it is a ludicrous fantasy. It would be simply and obviously idiotic to waste time torturing the "suspect" to find out in which of several schools the bomb was – even assuming for the moment that 'the authorities' really did know that 'he' really did know in which school it had been planted – instead of getting on the phone to evacuate everyone from all the schools. Admittedly this is a particularly inept example, offered by someone who states in the same article, apparently without the slightest irony, that it is often the case nowadays that some, like the United States military, take seriously those ethical restraints on war-fighting derived from the just or justified war tradition and encoded in various international conventions and agreements. Others may ignore these restraints. Nevertheless, those restraints – most importantly *noncombatant immunity* – are central to the way the United States makes war. [10]

But the carelessness of the example is by no means exceptional, as we shall see.

What seems even more remarkable, though, is that so many *opponents* of interrogational torture appear not to have given much more thought to the "facts" of the ticking bomb scenario examples than its supporters (whether with or without a warrant). It seems that its careless use by philosophers engaged in thought-experiments to test moral theory has had a profound effect even on those who offer a detailed critique of other aspects of this sort of argument.

Here is Jonathan Allen, an otherwise clear and robust critic of interrogational torture:

> In my view, torture may be an excusable tragic choice in very extreme circumstances. These circumstances are likely to be so rare that they do not justify taking the risks involved in incorporating torture within the legal system. Rather, officials who do torture in order to avert serious harms must face public scrutiny and penalties – even when we have good reason to think that they acted out of concern for public security. In some (but certainly not all) cases, those penalties would presumably be suspended, or would be minimal, or pardons would be granted. But the general prohibition against torture would be upheld. [11]

But if there really are some circumstances where torture is justifiable, albeit rarely, does not the 'general prohibition' survive only thanks to that rarity? And when the extraordinary becomes less so, the prohibition becomes increasingly precarious. Or consider Henry Shue, one of the foremost academic opponents of torture over the past twenty-five years:

> Nevertheless, it cannot be denied that there are imaginable cases in which the harm that could be prevented by a rare instance of pure interrogational torture would be so enormous as to outweigh the cruelty

of the torture itself and, possibly, the enormous potential harm which would result if what was intended to be a rare instance was actually the breaching of the dam which would lead to a torrent of torture. There is a standard philosopher's example which someone always invokes: suppose a fanatic, perfectly willing to die rather than collaborate in the thwarting of his own scheme, has set a hidden nuclear device to explode in the heart of Paris. There is no time to evacuate the innocent people or even the movable art treasures – the only hope of preventing a tragedy is to torture the perpetrator, find the device, and deactivate it.

I can see no way to deny the permissibility of torture in a case *just like this*. [12]

Shue goes on to argue that although 'If the example is made sufficiently extraordinary, the conclusion that the torture is permissible is secure', nonetheless 'one cannot easily draw conclusions for ordinary cases from extraordinary ones'. [13] Nor does 'the possibility that torture might be justifiable in some of the rarefied situations which can be imagined . . . provide any reason to consider relaxing the legal prohibitions against' torture. [14] But the problem is what counts as 'sufficiently extraordinary' or as 'rarefied'. Others are considerably less impressed by the 'extraordinary' nature of the philosophical example as a real-world possibility. Indeed, the extraordinary, they argue, has become all too everyday.

The rarity of the extraordinary is too precarious a basis for objections to interrogational torture. Once the concession is made that it might very, very occasionally be justified, in certain rare but not impossible cases, then all that stands in the way of justifying interrogational torture is the world's slowness in providing the requisite scenarios. And when that changes, whether in reality or in people's perception of reality, then interrogational torture comes to be seen as justified. The scene is now set for arguing either that it is morally justified and ought therefore to be legalized; or that, while morally objectionable, it ought nonetheless to be legalized; or that, while it is morally justified, it should remain illegal.

It is worth pointing out in passing that it is unclear whether Shue's point is that torture is justified if the example is made sufficiently *unusual*, or if it is made sufficiently *plausible* as a possibility: the phrase 'sufficiently extraordinary' remains ambiguous. Depending on whether he would take the first or the second view about 'how unlike the circumstances of an actual choice about torture the philosopher's example is', [15] he could be making either claim. But they are very different. And while it is all too easy quite unintentionally to move between these two different senses of 'extraordinary' – perhaps even more so in the heat of public debate than in academic exchange – that is all the more reason to avoid ambiguity. Whichever is in the end Shue's view, the question is not degree of unusualness, but whether or not the example *can* be made sufficiently plausible.

To clarify why that is the important question, let me return for a moment to the charge of hypocrisy. You might think that something morally right should nonetheless remain illegal, on the grounds that the likely consequences of its legalization are morally undesirable. Consider voluntary euthanasia, for example. As things currently stand, it might be thought that it were better that the practice, while morally right – even laudable – remain illegal, for fear of embarking on a slippery slope; and that we should continue to rely on the good sense of jurors not to convict even where it is clear that the accused did in fact assist someone to die. This is clearly Shue's position regarding interrogational torture:

> An act of torture ought to remain illegal so that anyone who sincerely believes such an act to be the least available evil is placed in the position of needing to justify his or her act morally in order to defend himself or herself legally. The torturer should be in roughly the same position as someone who commits civil disobedience. [16]

Now, that certainly escapes Dershowitz's charge of hypocrisy. Allen and Shue think that while interrogational torture might be morally justified "in principle and at the extreme", its remaining illegal is also morally justified – in fact, it is morally *demanded*. Like Dershowitz's, their reasoning is consequentialist. Where they differ from him is in their assessment of the likely consequences of legalization. Their position may be succinctly summed up by what Antony Flew argued some thirty years ago: 'If and when the conceivable, but in practice extremely rare, exceptional case occurs, the case in which torture actually would be justified, then let it be against the law that it is done, if it is done'. [17] Because of what I think would be the consequences of institutionalizing, and thus normalizing, interrogational torture, I agree with Allen, Shue and Flew about its legalization, as I shall argue in chapter three.

But that is not enough. It is *torture* and its acceptance that is the fundamental point, not its legalization. Objections to its legalization, then, are to the point only insofar as they constitute objections to one particular form – the most significant form, certainly – of its routinization, normalization or institutionalization. We need to take the ticking bomb scenario apart and to expose its internal structure, rather than just taking comfort from its rarity. For as Richard Jackson reminds us in his analysis of the language of 'the discursive construction of torture in the war on terrorism': while 'In fact, administration officials would have known that in thousands of cases of torture under similar presumptions, from Algeria to Israel, no bomb has ever been found', nonetheless, 'The internal logic of the discourse (however,) means that such knowledge is discounted in favour of a predetermined course of action'. [18] It is precisely that 'internal logic' which needs to be unpicked if the proposal to legalize interrogational torture is to be defeated, rather than becoming the new reality.

Who Tortures?

The first question, then, is this: is the so-called ticking bomb scenario in fact on a par with the train-driver example? Is it really an example of the "trolley problem"? I do not think it is. To see why, let us consider just a few more examples of its careless invocation. First, Anthony Quinton, writing in 1971:

> I do not see on what basis anyone could argue that the prohibition of torture is an absolute moral principle. . . . Consider a man caught planting a bomb in a large hospital, which no one dare touch for fear of setting it off. It was this kind of extreme situation I had in mind when I said earlier that I thought torture could be justifiable. [19]

Oddly, Quinton himself sees the obvious problem, but fails to see that it rules out just the sort of example he puts forward. He rightly points out that 'any but the most sparing recourse to [torture] will nourish a guild of professional torturers, a persisting danger to society much greater, even if more long-drawn-out, than anything their employment is likely to prevent'; and that 'If a society does not professionalize torture, then the limits of its efficiency make its application in any particular extreme situation that much more dubious'. The inevitable 'limits of its efficiency', however, do not *'make its application . . . much more dubious'* (my emphasis); [20] *they rule such application out*, simply because the ticking bomb scenario requires just that efficiency which the amateur torturer could not bring to it. The train driver is a train driver, not a trained torturer. Nor are Dershowitz's students. Nor is Dershowitz or other lawyers or philosophers. Nor are you. Nor am I. The first reason why the ticking bomb scenario remains a fantasy, and not a description of a rare but realistic possibility, is that it fails to distinguish between what you or I *might* do in that imagined case and what you or I *could* do in an actual case. It fails to distinguish between individuals' possible visceral responses and any proper basis of public policy.

The occasional advocates of torture in the 1980s – Gary Jones, [21] Michael Levin [22] – also blithely failed to distinguish between "us" and the professional torturers required actually to do the torturing. The tradition continues. Here is Fritz Allhoff, more recently:

> For example, imagine that we have just captured a high ranking official with an internationally known terrorist group and that our intelligence has revealed that this group has planted a bomb in a crowded office building that will likely explode tomorrow. This explosion will generate excessive civilian casualties and economic expense. We have a bomb squad prepared to move on the location when it is given, and there is plenty of time for them to disarm the bomb before its explosion tomorrow. We have asked this official for the location of the bomb, and he has refused to give it. Given these circumstances (which satisfy all four of my criteria), I think that it would be justifiable to torture the official in order to obtain the location of the bomb. [23]

Again, who are the 'we' who have captured this person and asked them where the bomb is? Is it the same 'we' who are to carry out the torture? The ready acceptance of the ticking bomb scenario without distinguishing between what you or I *might do* in that imagined case, what you or I *could do* in an actual case and what *"someone" would be expected to do* in an actual case has been both disastrous and unnecessary. Its irresponsible use by philosophers engaged in thought-experiments to test moral theory has had a profound effect even on those who offer a detailed critique of other aspects of this sort of argument. Even Jean Arrigo, Seth Kreimer, Barrie Paskins and Christopher

Tindale – all trenchant critics of the permissibility of interrogational torture, as we shall go on to see – overlook *this* fundamental flaw in the imagined scenario. Perhaps Michael Walzer's is the most galling example. In a recent interview, conducted in 2003, he quite reasonably objects to Dershowitz's use of his (Walzer's) treatment of "the problem of dirty hands" to justify torture warrants because 'extreme cases make bad law', yet immediately goes on to accept the case itself, apparently without noticing exactly what he is committing himself to: '[Yes], I would do whatever was necessary to extract information in the ticking bomb case – that is, I would make the same argument after 9/11 that I made 30 years before. But I do not want to generalize from cases like that; I don't want to rewrite the rule against torture to incorporate this exception.' [24] Or has Walzer recently undertaken torture training?

Nor is it just philosophers and the lawyers in their wake who indulge their thinking in this way. Here is Roy Hattersley, a British government minister, later to become Deputy Leader of the Labour Party (now thankfully thoroughly disillusioned):

> Let's imagine 250 people in an aeroplane, let's say we know some ter-
> rorists mean business because one bomb has gone off already, let's
> assume we've got a man and could save twenty-two odd lives by finding
> out where the second bomb is. If he wouldn't tell me I'd have to think
> very hard before I said don't bring any pressure to bear on that man
> that might cause him pain. [25]

At least Hattersley might be interpreted as half-seeing the problem, however. Despite the empirical oddities of his example, he distinguishes – whether entirely knowingly or not – between the man's telling *'me'* and his not saying, *presumably to someone else*, 'don't bring any pressure to bear . . . '.

You or I can imaginatively, and reasonably, put ourselves in the position of Dershowitz's train driver, at least to the extent of knowing how to operate the controls so as to 'swerve onto another track'. But we cannot put ourselves in the position of a torturer, and for two reasons. First, there is the sort and the precision of the skills required; second, and far more importantly, there is the question of the depths to which the acquisition and practice of such skills requires the torturer to sink. One need only read Ronald Crelinsten's discussion of how torturers are recruited and trained, for instance, [26] to realize the absurdity of asking the question, 'What would *you* do in a "ticking bomb" case?' Even if "you" were there when the person "you" knew to know where the bomb was, "you" would not know what to do. So I have to say that if "you" were an advocate either directly of the use of torture in such cases or of its legalization, you might have been expected to take into account such basic factual considerations. The train driver example and the ticking bomb scenario are radically different cases. The ticking bomb scenario requires us not to imagine what *we* would do, but to imagine what we would require *someone else* – a professional torturer – to do on our behalf; and not, furthermore, as an act of supererogation or altruism, but as the practice of their profession.

The institutionalization of the profession of torturer is a necessary condition of the example's even getting off the ground; and I shall pursue that in the next chapter. First, however, there are several other basic flaws in the ticking bomb scenario that need to be exposed.

Effectiveness and Time

Does torture work? We know that it is all too often effective in punishing, humiliating and terrorizing both the person under torture and others. The history of the second half of the twentieth century in Central and South America, the Middle East, Africa and the Far East is testament to that. [27] But that is not the issue here. The issue is whether or not it is an effective means of obtaining information. There are in turn two questions here. Is it effective in eliciting general and/or background intelligence? Is it effective in "ticking bomb" circumstances?

Field Manual 34–52, the rulebook of American military interrogators, 'prohibits the use of coercive techniques because they produce low quality intelligence': 'The use of force is a poor technique, as it yields unreliable results, may damage subsequent collection efforts, and can induce the source to say whatever he [*sic*] thinks the interrogator wants to hear'. [28] Dershowitz, on the contrary, argues that 'It is precisely because torture sometimes does work and can prevent major disasters that it still exists in many parts of the world and has been totally eliminated from none'. [29] He offers no direct argument against the claims of the American *Field Manual*, however, an omission which in the circumstances appears odd. For the *Field Manual* is not alone in its conclusion. Here is Cyril Cunningham, for example, a psychologist with British Intelligence, writing to *The Times* already in 1971 about the "physical and psychological pressure" used by British forces in Northern Ireland:

> If the Royal Ulster Constabulary, or indeed the Army, is using the methods reported, they are being singularly stupid and unimaginative. . . . A variety of "backdoor" methods are available, all of which depend for their effectiveness upon the avoidance of brutality in any form. [30]

Across the world, those who have the best claim to know – the military – agree that torture is largely ineffective in eliciting intelligence. That is why the latest version (at the time of writing) of the US *Field Manual*, updated in response to the Abu Ghraib scandal, is not alone in underlining the point. [31]

But what about the specific circumstances of a "ticking bomb"? Such evidence as we have is, inevitably, anecdotal and contradictory. For instance, I have personally been told that members of the Israeli security forces have claimed that a bomb was found and defused as a result of torturing the person who had planted it. [32] On the other hand, such claims are also denied. I shall return to this issue presently.

What is striking, however, is that Dershowitz's own examples, of Egypt and Jordan, to whom of course 'the US government sometimes "renders" terrorist suspects', [33] are not remotely of the ticking bomb variety. Nor is it interrogational torture to prevent an imminent disaster that is being described by the French general, 'Paul Aussaresses, [who] wrote a book recounting what he had done and seen, including the torture of dozens of Algerians. "The best way to make a terrorist talk when he refused to say what he knew was to torture him," he boasted.' [34] Dershowitz's examples of Abu Nidal and the 1993 World Trade Center attacks in his *explicit* defence of the claim 'that torture sometimes works, even if it does not always work', [35] furthermore, are conspicuous by the enormity of their difference from that of the ticking bomb scenario. Here is what he says: 'There can be no doubt that torture sometimes works. Jordan apparently broke the most notorious terrorist of the 1980s, Abu Nidal, *by threatening his mother.* Philippine police reportedly helped crack the 1993 World Trade Center bombings by torturing a suspect' (my emphasis). [36] The first case is *obviously not* one where physically torturing a terrorist, or terrorist suspect, worked; it was when his mother was threatened that Abu Nidal 'broke', which is quite another matter (as I shall elaborate below). And in neither case was there a ticking bomb waiting to be defused. Even stranger in the context of a ticking bomb is his citing this report (which I shall assume for the sake of argument is accurate):

> There are numerous instances in which torture has produced self-proving, truthful information that was necessary to prevent harm to civilians. The *Washington Post* has recounted a case from 1995 in which Philippine authorities tortured a terrorist into disclosing information that may have foiled plots to assassinate the pope and to crash eleven commercial airliners carrying approximately four thousand passengers into the Pacific ocean, as well as a plan to fly a private Cessna filled with explosives into CIA headquarters. For sixty-seven days, intelligence agents beat the suspect. . . . [37]

Sixty-seven days? So what on earth has this report to do with any *ticking bomb*, or with any imminent catastrophe?

So much for Dershowitz's supporting arguments about the effectiveness of torture in cases where time really is of the essence. As for threats against a prisoner's mother, suffice it to say for the moment that, if carried out, it would directly contradict Dershowitz's avowed objection to torturing a third party, rather than the person purportedly known actually to have the information. (Of course, such a threat may itself be regarded as a form of torture; but that is clearly not what he has in mind, either explicitly – 'a sterilized needle inserted under the finger-nails' [38] – or implicitly, since its credibility would depend on the authorities being prepared to carry the threat out.) I shall return to this in the next chapter.

Still, the only evidence available about real ticking bomb cases is anecdotal and thus inconclusive. So the best we can do is to try to think through what might reasonably be expected to happen in such a case. Accepting for the moment that the captive in question really does know where the bomb is, what is their likely strategy? Remember that it is only interrogational torture which is permitted; and remember also that part of the case for legalizing it is that doing so will help ensure that non-interrogational torture – as punishment, for example – will be more likely to be eliminated. The captive's position, then, is this. First, they know that unless they reveal where the bomb is, they will be (non-lethally) tortured. Second, they know that the torture will cease immediately they give the information required. Third, they know that, since the torture will also cease immediately the bomb explodes, the time for which they have to endure the torture is comparatively short. After all, the legal conditions surrounding torture, and in particular its being limited to interrogational torture, are something any likely terrorist would have very good reason to know, as Dershowitz himself rightly recognizes: 'the torturee will know that there are limits to the torture being inflicted'. [39] How short that time will be, neither we, the interrogators, the torturers, nor anyone else knows; but the captive does, since that is part of the scenario. But it will certainly be short: 'if they know about the bomb, they'll know how long they have got to hold out, which gives them an important psychological advantage'. [40] Furthermore, realistically and unsurprisingly, bombers are going to leave as little time as possible between planting the bomb and its going off, precisely so as to avoid "premature" discovery. In light of all that, the captive's tactic is obvious: 'Terrorists willing to die for their cause would also be willing to plant false tales under torture', [41] as John Langbein, the eminent legal historian of torture, succinctly puts it. The point is that the already 'guilty terrorist' [42] – who is most unlikely to be the crazed fanatic, unable to act rationally, of popular misrepresentation – is rather more dedicated and determined than you or I.

Furthermore, anyone planting a bomb is likely to have undergone training in resisting torture (in the knowledge that it is likely to be applied, should they be caught in these circumstances) and is likely to have their wits about them. Again, what will they do? Their first recourse, surely, is to prevaricate, and deny knowing where the bomb is. They would also be well advised to try to persuade their interrogators that *someone else* knows where it is. Certainly they could buy precious time by persuading interrogators to seek a torture warrant for someone else. But let us assume, perhaps reasonably, that such a tactic would not last very long. Or, perhaps no less realistically, if somewhat generously, we could assume that the captive would calculate that it was not a tactic worth trying, since they knew that the interrogators knew that they knew where the bomb was. The interrogators had, after all, persuaded the relevant authorities to issue a torture warrant on the basis of the evidence of such knowledge. What now? The critical issue here is time. And again, one pretty obvious way of buying time in *these* circumstances is simply to lie about the whereabouts of the bomb, and in as complicated a way as possible, hoping that by the time their lie was discovered, the bomb would be that much closer to going off – and the (now resumed) torture, remember, therefore that much closer to stopping.

In fact, why not lie repeatedly? The interrogators cannot know they are being lied to until the location given is checked out; and every location stated has to be checked out, just in case it turns out to be the real one. In light of this obvious point, it is perhaps not surprising that none of those who argue that interrogational torture is justifiable tell us whether or not they think the torture ought to stop while the stated location is checked out. For if it did stop, the "suspect's" best strategy is obvious, perhaps even making difficult the *systematic* infliction of pain that torture consists in. And if the torture really were to remain solely interrogational, note, the torture would *have* to stop while the authorities checked the captive's story – however cynical you might be about interrogators actually behaving in such a "gentlemanly" way, or about observers insisting on this condition. On the other hand, if for just that reason the argument were that the torture should not stop while the story was checked out, then we have something rather different from purely *interrogational* torture: practically speaking, an element of torturing "just in case" ineluctably appears. And if that is justified here, why not elsewhere? Why not torture people whom the authorities have reason to think *might* know where the bomb is?

Then there is also the likelihood of lying out of desperation, rather than deliberately misleading the interrogators. That likelihood increases in direct proportion to the degree of pain inflicted: the closer the pain is to being literally unbearable, the greater the incentive to say just anything at all to bring it to an end. And of course, the less time there is, the more likely that would be to work as a tactic anyway. So for both reasons – desperation and tactics – the more urgent the situation, and thus the more justified the torture and the warrant authorizing it, the smaller the chance of stopping the bomb going off. Conversely, the greater that chance, the less urgent the situation. But it is urgency that is said to justify the torture. No wonder there is a general, if not of course unanimous, agreement, reflected in the *Field Manual* referred to above, that information given under torture is unreliable.

I am not saying that these reflections show that torture cannot possibly be effective in the ticking bomb scenario; only that the evidence offered, such as it is, fails to take any cognisance of obvious practical objections. What we are being invited to weigh, therefore, is *not* the torture of one person against the death and maiming of hundreds, or even thousands, of innocent civilians (and allowing for the moment an unfounded confidence that we know they are indeed a 'guilty terrorist'). It is, rather, the torture of that person against the *possibility* of the death and maiming of hundreds, or even thousands, of innocent civilians. How high is that possibility? We do not know. But what we do know is this. If you agree with the utilitarian approach on which the argument is based, then, the higher you think the possibility is of death and mutilation, the more heavily you will take it to weigh on the side of torture; and the lower you think it is, the less heavily you will take it to weigh. So unless you do know what the possibility is, at least roughly, you *cannot* be in a position to judge its weight against torture. Your position therefore has to be that torture is justified by even the possibility of catastrophe – not by its certainty.

Interestingly, Dershowitz himself acknowledges the empirical difficulty, even if he resolutely ignores its implications. In a footnote to the sentence above where he states that 'torture *sometimes* works', and in which he offers the examples of Abu Nidal's mother and the World Trade Center bombings, he concedes, as we have already seen, that 'It is of course possible that judicially supervised torture will work less effectively than unsupervised torture, since the torturee will know that there are limits to the torture being inflicted. At this point in time, any empirical resolution of this issue seems speculative.' [43] Indeed so. But then on what grounds exactly *does* Dershowitz think that the balance of judgement *just obviously* lies on the side of interrogational torture? And why does he *not* consider either the implications of his own empirical caveat or the claims of the US *Field Manual* and other counter-evidence?

Furthermore, if there really is good reason to suppose that there is a bomb about to go off very soon – but not so soon as to make torture impractical – and the available professional techniques of torture are sufficiently refined and effective to offer a realistic prospect of rapid success, then, as Levinson points out, 'anyone who believes that torture is acceptable with a warrant would, I suspect, waive the requirement when time is truly of the essence'. [44] Again, it is curious that Dershowitz does not address this point in his published writing. [45] Nor is that all. To the extent that time really was pressing, then, as Allen reminds us, 'it seems all too likely that a genuinely stringent process of scrutiny would slow the process down to the point of ineffectiveness. . . . it would take time to compile evidence, and time for judges to sift through it (and even) [I]f authority to issue warrants was reserved to a small set of highly qualified judges, it might well be difficult to obtain rapid access to (them)'. [46] Or to put it rather more bluntly: these are 'classic cases of emergency or exigent circumstances in which the police generally do not have time to obtain warrants'. [47] For 'the court hearing the warrant application will scarcely have more time to make the decision than the front-line official confronted with the problem at first instance. In making this decision, the court will need information, which means that the applicant will need time to prepare materials.' [48] And even after that delay, the more deeply a conscientious judge inquires as to whether or not the matter really is sufficiently urgent, the more time will turn out to have been wasted if it does turn out to be urgent. On the other hand, the louder the ticking, so to speak, the less time for a judge to consider the matter. Under these inevitable counter-pressures, it is a reasonable expectation that judges' default position would be to issue a warrant lest it turn out that they be accused of having blood on their hands.

One has to ask if it is the lack of realism about time in real cases that allows advocates of torture also not to consider empirical issues about the efficacy of other methods of interrogation. [49] A reasonable response would of course be that we are dealing with extremely determined people, on whom such "softer" methods would be extremely unlikely to work; or that we could give such methods a quick try, perhaps while the authorities are considering whether or not to issue a warrant. The argument is that torture is the ultimate weapon against determination. But then as I have indicated, the argument just *assumes* that torture is sufficiently likely to be effective; it appeals to examples quite different from interrogational torture in ticking bomb scenarios; and it fails to offer remotely adequate positive evidence.

The more closely one tries actually to specify the time conditions of the ticking bomb case, the more the reality obtrudes against the fantasy of the thought-experiment. Unsurprisingly, perhaps, it was a serving American soldier, Major William Casebeer, who made the central point of which advocates of interrogational torture appear so disconcertingly unaware:

> The imminence of the danger requirement will probably only be met in radically underspecified thought-experiments like the ticking bomb scenario (indeed, the very intelligence that will enable us to know we are facing an imminent danger will also likely serve to give us means to discover the source of the danger without having to resort to torture interrogation). [50]

Knowledge and Necessity

We have already seen that it is an assumption that interrogators know that their captive has the information they are after, that they are 'guilty' before any legal process which might establish their guilt. Now of course it is *possible* that the person concerned has admitted planting the bomb or knowing where someone else has planted it; or that the authorities really do know, from surveillance perhaps, that the captive knows where the bomb is (see chapter four). We are dealing not with a thought-experiment, however, but with reality. We have to take into account just how likely it is that the interrogators have the requisite knowledge.

Jonathan Allen sets out the situation regarding knowledge succinctly:

> for the "ticking bomb" scenario to constitute a truly compelling case for torture, we would have to know: (a) that we are holding the right person; (b) that the person being tortured really does possess the information we need; (c) that acquiring the information the captured terrorist possesses would be very likely to put us in a position to avert a disaster, and that his accomplices haven't already adopted a contingency plan he knows nothing about; (d) that the information we obtain through torture is reliable.
>
> We can of course stipulate that we know these things – and if we do, we really are presented with an important test of the validity of moral absolutism. *However, in reality, we will be operating to a greater or lesser degree on the basis of supposition, not certainty* [my emphasis]. [51]

Citing the case of Paul Teitgen during the Algerian war of liberation, Allen reminds us that 'real cases, even those that approximate the "ticking bomb" scenario, involve much more uncertainty, and therefore require complex judgements'. [52] Even Levinson, who reluctantly semi-endorses Dershowitz's proposal – since we 'are staring into an abyss, and no one can escape the necessity of a response' [53] – notes that 'there is no known example of this actually occurring, in the sense of having someone in custody who knew of a bomb likely to go off within the hour'. [54] And as we have seen, all Dershowitz offers is the unreferenced claim that in Israel 'There is little doubt that some acts of terrorism – which would have killed many civilians – were prevented. There is also little doubt that the cost of saving these lives – measured in terms of basic human rights – was extraordinarily high.' [55] As against that, consider for example Alisa Solomon's comment on the sort of claim that people certainly *make* – and not only Dershowitz – but one which, to my knowledge, remains *unsubstantiated*:

> The Israelis made much use of their ability to use "moderate physical pressure" to save hundreds of lives in "ticking bomb" cases – that is, on occasions when a confession can lead directly to the prevention of an imminent attack. Nonetheless, according to Dr. Ruchama Marton, the founder of Israel's Physicians for Human Rights and coeditor of *Torture: Human Rights, Medical Ethics and the Case of Israel*, even the staunchest defenders of the most aggressive interrogation methods never provided details of a single specific case in which torture led to the immediate deactivating of a ticking bomb. [56]

Now of course to quote someone who, like Dr Marton, may reasonably be taken to be an authority on the matter, is not to substantiate Solomon's claim. Nonetheless, one can at least check the source, compare it with other sources and so on. What strikes me as significant here is not only that Dershowitz appears to rely on unsubstantiated hearsay, but that when he goes on to make an argument on the basis of it two pages later, he quotes Jeremy Bentham's discussion of interrogational torture. And what Bentham says there is very different indeed from Dershowitz's own stipulation, in the form of a quotation from Twining and Twining (which he gives another two pages further on) that 'The evidence in support of the contention that he has the relevant information would satisfy the requirements of evidence for *convicting him of an offence'* (my emphasis). [57] What Bentham says, and what Dershowitz correctly quotes him as saying, is this: 'Suppose an occasion were to arise, in which a suspicion is entertained, as strong as that which would be received as a sufficient ground for *arrest and commitment as for felony . . .'* (my emphasis). [58] And that is very far indeed from knowing that the captive has the information, that they are a 'guilty terrorist'. Evidence sufficient to convict is one thing; evidence sufficient to arrest is quite another. Nor is he alone here. Others who countenance torture *in extremis* are even more vague. Walzer, for example, whom Dershowitz quotes, [59] writes of authorizing 'the torture of a captured rebel leader who *knows or probably knows* the location of a number of bombs' (my emphasis). [60] In a matter as serious as this, such laxity is irresponsible, to say the least.

The empirical question of how likely it is that a given captive has the requisite knowledge remains uncertain. So, to extend the earlier points about the efficacy of torture and the time element in the ticking bomb scenario – and remembering that putative bomb-planters know that being captured before the bomb goes off will lead to torture – the question to be asked is this. How likely is it that someone *already* in custody is the bomb-planter, or a sufficiently close associate of the bomb-planter, to know where the bomb is? People who plant bombs will, after all, have taken care to leave as little time as possible between planting the bomb and its going off. Unless they had already been under surveillance, therefore, their being taken into custody in the interval between planting and explosion must be extraordinarily unlikely; and of course, if they had been under surveillance, then those conducting the surveillance would be very likely to know where the bomb was or who the person was who knew where it was. Elaine Scarry's comment is exactly to the point, even if 'highly improbable' turns out to be an understatement, since it is not only knowing that the detainee knows what the ticking bomb scenario has them know that is the problem:

> What makes it improbable is not the existence of a ticking bomb (it is entirely possible that a terrorist or a deranged state leader will one day try to use a nuclear bomb, or a chemical or biological weapon capable of killing hundreds of thousands). What instead makes the ticking bomb scenario improbable is the notion that in a world where knowledge is ordinarily so imperfect, we are suddenly granted the

omniscience to know that the person in front of us holds this crucial information about the bomb's whereabouts. [61]

To put it succinctly: 'we cannot usually be certain of guilt if we do not have all the information. If we did have it, we would not be tempted to resort to torture.' [62] In the United States, as Scarry goes on to point out, 'In the two and a half years since September 11, 2001[at the time of writing], five thousand foreign nationals suspected of being terrorists have been detained without access to counsel, only three of whom have ever eventually been charged with terrorism-related acts; two of those three have been acquitted'. [63] Or consider the case of Ziad Mustafa Al-Zaghal, whom 'six persons' accused of being an active member of 'an Islamic military organization' and of whom the legal representative of the GSS (in the case he brought against it) stated that he was a man 'who if he talks under interrogation, can prevent bombings': after five months of detention without charges or trial, he was released, having not been 'accused of any offense' – 'the "six persons" were not brought to testify that Al-Zaghal was "active in a military organization" or planned any time of bombings [sic]'. [64] Again, as Arrigo asks, 'What proportion of ignorant or innocent suspects are likely to be interrogated under torture? Modern crime statistics indicate that among suspects arrested and charged with serious crimes, one-half to three-quarters are not convicted, depending on the [US] state of jurisdiction.' [65] So how likely is it that in the ticking bomb scenario the authorities should come to be blessed with the near-omniscience they lack elsewhere?

Let me sum up. If anyone really intends torture warrants to be issued only in those cases where it is as certain as it empirically can be that the person to be tortured has the relevant knowledge, then the onus is on them to establish how we may achieve such certainty. So far as I know, no one has done so. Given the obvious empirical obstacles I have outlined, that omission seriously undermines the ticking bomb scenario.

Its whole point is to engender a sense of necessity: "the terrorist" *who knows where the bomb is* has to be tortured in order to prevent the death and maiming of thousands of innocent people. But what sort of necessity is this? How do we know that the torture is necessary, that the disaster is imminent and unavoidable other than through the use of torture – or rather, as imminent as my earlier qualifications allow?

The situations said to demand torture warrants are extremely likely to be underdetermined in respect of its being known whether or not the person to be tortured actually does know what it is proposed to torture them to find out. And the more closely specified the example is, so as to make such knowledge plausible, the less persuasive it is as one describing a real situation.

Now, it could be said in reply that *of course* empirical knowledge can never be certain, and that talk of the necessity of torture is to be understood as using an ordinary, everyday sense of 'necessary', and not some theoretical (or philosophical) sense of the word.

> 'It's raining: you need to take your umbrella or you'll get wet.' That's what I mean by its being 'necessary' to use torture here. Unless you use torture, you won't get the information – which is not to say that even if you do use it, you'll *certainly* get it. As I've already said, 'No technique of crime prevention always works.' [66]

That is an entirely fair point. But precisely because it is, precisely because certainty is unavailable, what we are actually being invited to accept is that interrogational torture is morally justifiable because it *might* – and, if my arguments so far are right, *only just might* – avoid the catastrophe. What is at issue here is the possibility of having the knowledge that time is sufficiently short to make the case a matter of necessity; and this takes us back to my earlier discussion of time and effectiveness. If it is not *known* that time is (sufficiently) short, then it cannot be *known* that the case is a matter of necessity, and that there is therefore not time to try techniques such as "talking the suspect down". How then does the interrogator know that time is (sufficiently) short? It is logically possible that the detainee has told them – but of course the knowledge that the interrogators' knowing this leads to torture would make this even less likely than it already is. Can anyone seriously imagine a prisoner's admitting that there is a bomb set to go off at a particular time but then adamantly refusing to say where it is, knowing that they will be tortured to make them give that information? [67] As we have seen, it is obviously in such a person's interest to know what the law allows and what it does not. The knowledge that torture would follow from such an admission would make it even more unlikely than it already is in the absence of such a threat that they would make the original admission. Perhaps, though, someone else has told them that there is such a bomb, that they themselves do not know where it is, but that they do know that this other person knows where it is. But then how do the interrogators, or the authorities charged with issuing or withholding a torture warrant, know that *that* information is reliable? Again, it is inordinately unlikely, to say the least, that the interrogator would have the knowledge that is a logical condition of invoking necessity.

To argue, then, that the ticking bomb scenario is one where torture is *necessary* is misleading. It is only in the everyday sense that we can, in the real world, say in advance that something or other is necessary. But in that case all we really mean is that, for example, taking an umbrella is *one* way of not getting wet. You could take a mac; or you could stay at home. You could also choose to get wet. The necessity of torture in a particular instance, as the *only* possible solution, cannot be known in advance. That is why the ticking bomb scenario must remain radically underspecified. Probability is all there can be in the matter; and probability, not being certainty, raises three issues.

First, how strong a probability would be required to generate a torture warrant? If the standard were set too high – say 99 per cent – then the whole practical point of legalizing interrogational torture would disappear. As Dershowitz rightly insists, no legal sanctions or processes are 100 per cent effective. Perhaps, then, a 90 per cent likelihood would be sufficient. But in that case, why not 89 per cent? After all, the circumstances of the "ticking bomb" are so extreme as to justify what even the advocates of torture and/or its legalization agree to be a last resort. The point is that the more convincing the urgency of the scenario, the lower it makes sense to set the threshold of torture. So why not 51 per cent? Or less? The structure of the proposal leads remorselessly to the conclusion that torture warrants would come to be issued where there *might* be a bomb shortly to go off; where there *might* be a bomb which *might* be shortly to go off; and where that 'shortly' *might* be so short that torture was the only possible means of avoiding the catastrophe. Torture warrants would rapidly come to be issued routinely, just because torture *might* be needed. What follows from this, is that, second, there cannot but be some risk, in all probability an increasingly considerable risk, of torturing the wrong person, or of torturing a person when torture might not have been necessary after all. As Scarry says, 'When we imagine the ticking bomb situation, does our imaginary omniscience enable us to get the information by torturing one person? Or will the numbers more closely resemble the situation of the [five thousand] detainees: we will be certain, and incorrect, 4,999 times that we stand in the presence of someone with the crucial data, and only get it right with the five thousandth prisoner?' [68] Third, as we have already seen, we cannot be sure that the torture will work: 'success is being assumed and not demonstrated', since, as again Tindale points out, 'Viewed prospectively, the guarantee of success cannot be assumed. The terrorist may withstand whatever humane or inhumane treatment is applied or may give misleading information that will be time-consuming to check.' [69]

The "necessity" that gives the thought experiment its force is inevitably absent in the real case. In the real world, necessity is always retrospective. Anat Biletzki makes this abundantly clear in the course of her analysis of the Israeli Supreme Court's 1999 ruling against interrogational torture: 'the "necessity" defense is an after-the-fact judgement, useful and relevant in cases where an investigator is accused of wrong-doing. It cannot function as a normative, before-the-fact guide to anything'. [70] No wonder that the best evidence Dershowitz can cite is that 'the Israeli security services *claimed* that, as a result of the Supreme Court's decision, at least one preventable act of terrorism had been allowed to take place, one that killed several people when a bus was bombed' (my emphasis). In fairness, he clearly recognizes the shortcoming: 'Whether this claim is true, false, or somewhere in between is difficult to assess', [71] he says. But yet again, what he does not recognize is the impact that that admission should have on his argument.

He points out, as we have seen, that we sanction other legal practices where success cannot be guaranteed and/or where we may inadvertently be committing an injustice against a particular individual. And certainly, he is right to point out that 'In the United States we execute convicted murderers, despite compelling evidence of the unfairness and ineffectiveness of capital punishment'. [72] But what he fails to consider, whether parochially, disingenuously or for some other reason, is that this argument can as easily be inverted: given 'compelling evidence of the unfairness and ineffectiveness of capital punishment', it should be abolished. Or again, 'imprisoning a witness who refuses to testify after being given immunity is designed to be punitive – that is painful', and success cannot be assured. [73] True enough: but imprisonment is hardly on a par with torture. Still, Dershowitz is right that in general ineffectiveness is no bar to penal practices: we know that in the UK the success rate of prison sentences in preventing youths reoffending is at best only round about 20 per cent, and that all too often innocent people are jailed, yet that does not lead most people to argue that these practices should be abandoned (whether or not it ought to). But that is not the point. The point is that the case for interrogational torture depends on such plausibility as some think it has on its *necessity* as a last resort, so that the more the claim regarding certainty of success is qualified, the weaker its justification. And it turns out that it *may be necessary* – that is all. Substitute this more cautious phrase in a ticking bomb scenario and any initial plausibility disappears.

The Ticking Bomb Scenario: Conclusion

The more closely the real case approximates to the ticking bomb fantasy, the closer it is to its being too late to prevent the impending catastrophe. By the time the "guilty" terrorist who has planted the bomb has been apprehended, then, if its going off really is imminent, it is too late. Arrigo brings a much-needed empirical realism to the fantasy:

> As a prototype to guide a torture interrogation program, the time scale of the ticking bomb scenario is extremely misleading. In FBI experience, deterrence of terrorist acts is a long-term affair, with informants, electronic surveillance networks, and undercover agents. Operations must be tracked and allowed to play out almost to the last stage to comprehend their scope. The fanatics, martyrs, and heroes scenario errs, like the ticking bomb scenario, in its focus on key terrorists. They are difficult to apprehend and likely to require great exertions from torturers. Their numerous peripheral associates are much easier to apprehend and more susceptible to interrogation – whence the inevitable trend towards the dragnet interrogation model of knowledge acquisition. Among the detainees will be many innocent or ignorant persons but these, too, are critical for comparison of nonterrorist with terrorist data. The difficulty 'from a purely intelligence point of view', as noted by Horne, is that 'more often than not the collating services are overwhelmed by a mountain of false information extorted from victims desperate to save themselves further agony'. [74]

The answer to the "tragic scenario" is that we need to do what we can to ensure that we never get anywhere near it. The proposal to legalize interrogational torture, in addition to all its other demerits, stands in the way of our succeeding in doing exactly that. Why should we think that legally torturing suspects would diminish, rather than increase, terrorist bombings, when the evidence we have – such as it is – of the effect of parallel legal measures (and of other related policies) in the so-called war on terror points in exactly the opposite direction? In appearing to offer a solution, this short cut would serve to deflect from the harder task of eliminating the causes of the putative incident where "we" are urged to resort to legal torture. Despite claiming the "realist" high ground, these arguments are firmly rooted in fantasy. And while, as Shue and others argue, hard cases make bad law, fantasy makes for something far worse. Maybe 'We can imagine and describe cases in which we would think torture justified and unjustified . . . (and) state the grounds on which we are making the distinction. But what we cannot do is this: *we cannot provide for ourselves, or for those who must act for us in real situations, any way of making our notional distinctions in reality'*. But even if Barrie Paskins is right in his first claim, the second destroys any plausibility that such cases might have as the basis of an argument about what ought to be done in real situations, where 'we can never be certain that the case in hand is of this kind rather than another'. [75]

Nowhere in *Why Terrorism Works* or anywhere else is there a draft wording, however embryonic, of the legislation proposed. That might seem surprising. But it is not. For any attempt legislatively to specify the circumstances in which such a warrant might be granted, the conditions governing who would grant it and to whom, and what it would permit and what not, would require a basis of just that realism which the ticking bomb scenario precludes. No wonder, then, that as Markus Wagner points out, Dershowitz prefers appeals to fantasies such as *Marathon Man* to saying anything realistic about 'the exact requirements for obtaining' such warrants. [76] Like so much of the rest of the so-called war on terrorism, the object of the proposal is a fantasy. [77]

Chapter Three

The Consequences of Normalizing Interrogational Torture

Here is Zvi Aharoni, head of interrogation in the Shabak (the Israeli security service) during the 1950s, speaking in 1997:

> I took part in building the internal security service and I was proud of it, of everything we did. Let me tell you one thing, when I was head of the interrogation department, nobody could touch a prisoner. Sure, you could do all kinds of tricks, you could bug them, listen in on their conversation. But beating them? Torturing them? And today not only is it being done, it's legal, Arabs can be tortured. It's legal and in my country. [1]

In this chapter, I shall try to show that Aharoni is right to be ashamed, not just of torture, but of its legalization; and not just because of his entirely appropriate revulsion, but because of the social consequences of legalizing interrogational torture. For even if I succeeded in persuading you in the last chapter that the ticking bomb scenario as presented by explicit advocates of interrogational torture and/or proponents of its legalization remains sheer fantasy, you may still have a nagging doubt that, nevertheless, *something* like it remains at least theoretically possible. So the question we have to think through is this: what exactly are the likely consequences of institutionalizing interrogational torture? After examining three positive claims made by advocates of legalizing interrogational torture, I shall go on to offer my own view of what would happen in the four central areas on which that would impact: the wider use of torture; its consequences for the law; the response of potential terrorist bombers; and the professionalization of torture.

Some Clarifications

But before going into those details, I need to clarify three things, so as to make clear the *sorts* of consequence at issue. First, I need to discuss the idea of institutionalizing a practice. Second, I need to develop what I said in the previous chapter about the difference between what you think of a practice and what you think of institutionalizing that practice. When considering social consequences, that is to say, we need to consider not only the substantial issue itself – in this case interrogational *torture* – but also what it is proposed to do about it – in this case *legalizing*, and thus *permitting* and *normalizing*, interrogational torture. Third, I need to disentangle what might perhaps still seem a paradox but is not: how can someone who advocates the legalization of interrogational torture nonetheless insist that they are morally opposed to torture? For that is certainly Dershowitz's position. It also represents in more explicit and exact form a general view held much more widely, by politicians, policy-makers and the public: of course torture is morally awful – but sometimes it is necessary.

Institutionalization

An institutionalized practice is one which is socially accepted, and thus in one sense socially acceptable – which is not to say that everyone finds it acceptable, of course. An obvious example is going to school; another is marriage, whether traditional or not. These are normal practices, normal in both senses of the word: they are common; and they are generally regarded as at least morally permissible, even if not by everyone. Thus drinking alcohol has long been institutionalized in western societies; gay marriage is on the way to being institutionalized in some of them; and smoking in public places is becoming unacceptable to the point of legal prohibition. Where hitherto a practice has been legally unauthorized, like gay marriage, or prohibited, like assisted suicide, it of course requires legislation to authorize it or overturn the prohibition. Generally, such legislation follows at least some increasing social acceptability. Consider the legalization in the United Kingdom of homosexual sex in the early 1960s, or that of abortion in 1967: both have now become institutionalized, which is to say they are an accepted facet of social life. One might say, then, that they have been normalized, in both the statistical and the moral sense of the term: what is *deemed* acceptable has come to be generally accepted. Thus many people whose visceral response thirty years ago to homosexuality would have been one of embarrassment, disapproval or disgust are no longer particularly bothered by it; and for younger generations it is simply not an issue. It has become normal.

Legislation, however, is not the only vehicle of normalization. Some practices come to be accepted as normal, to be institutionalized, in all sorts of other ways, and without being the subject of legislation, simply because they were never illegal, but merely unusual or unknown. Consider, for example, drinking wine with dinner or flying abroad on holiday: fifty years ago almost unkown in the UK, today these are commonplace. Or consider how talking on the phone in public has become routine. But these changes are not deliberate. No one decided that they should take place; they just happened. More significant practices tend to be normalized through legislation, however, simply because it is only such practices – sexual ones, for example – that will have been thought important enough to remain legally unauthorized or prohibited in the first place.

Some illegal practices, of course – accepting bribes in business deals, or voluntary euthanaesia – become institutionalized even though they remain illegal. They are accepted as statistically normal, as part of everyday life: everyone accepts that they occur. But they have not become *morally* normalized. Some people regard them as morally unacceptable; others do not concern themselves about their morality at all; and still others regard them as morally justified, whatever their legal status.

As things stand, torture comes into the first and second of these categories: most people think it is morally wrong, while others give it no moral thought at all. What advocates of interrogational torture are inviting us to do is to bring it into the third category, to accept that it is, in certain real cases, morally justified. Where they differ is this. While Dershowitz wants torture to be legalized either *because* interrogational torture is morally justified (most of his critics' understanding of what he says) or *because* its legalization is morally justified (which, he insists, is actually his position), most others, like Posner, want it to remain illegal *although* they think it is morally justified.

Practices and their institutionalization

A practice is one thing; what you think ought to be done about it is another. Why? Because the consequences of what you do or do not do about it also have moral and/or social consequences – whether desirable or undesirable. And these are different from considerations about the rightness or wrongness of the practice itself. They might be less important, as important or more important: but they are not the same. So, for example, legalizing prostitution might be expected to have certain effects on people's view of sex and of sexual relations; and conversely, so might making it illegal to buy, though not to sell, sexual services, effects which in turn would be very different from making it illegal to sell, though not to buy, sexual services. [2] A helpful way of talking about this is to refer to the impact that legalizing a practice has on the moral climate, on people's moral attitudes more generally. This sort of impact can be much wider than anything directly connected with the practice. You might object to sponsored runs for charities as being deeply misguided, because they encourage the erosion of collective social responsibility, and not because you think there is anything wrong with running *per se*. Furthermore, even if you do object, you might still think you ought to go along with sponsored runs despite their effect on collective social responsibility because of the consequences of not doing so – your friend's being upset, or people thinking you a crotchety old pedant who takes themselves and their views far too seriously. Or you might take a negative view of the institution of marriage, but still think that in certain cases you ought nonetheless to turn up to someone's wedding. In none of these cases need your moral judgement of a practice line up neatly with your judgement of what to do about it.

Let me make the distinction clearer with a few more examples. Suppose you think assisted suicide is right, and are even convinced that in certain circumstances you ought to help a close friend to kill themselves. Still, you might think *either* that, *because* giving such help is morally right, it ought to be made legal; *or* that, *although* it is morally right, nevertheless it ought to remain illegal. That is to say, you might think either that the law has no business forbidding what is right; or (perhaps while thinking also that *normally* the law has no such business) that legalizing assisted suicide would lead to all sorts of *other* morally objectionable states of affairs. Examples might be feelings of guilt on the part of people who do not want to take that way out; its being used by government as an excuse for not supporting hospices; or pressure being brought to bear by medical staff and family. And you might think that these harms outweigh the harm done by subjecting people to legal sanctions for doing something you think morally right (not least as we can generally rely on the good sense of a jury to acquit in such cases). [3] Or take cannabis: you might think the consequences of smoking cannabis, both individual and social, are no worse than those of smoking tobacco or drinking alcohol, and that it ought therefore to be legalized. You might equally believe the contrary: that although smoking cannabis is no worse than various other pleasures, legalizing it would be the first step on a slippery slope which would lead to the acceptance – and in the long run perhaps the legalization – of other drugs which really are harmful. Conversely, of course, you might disapprove of a practice, but nonetheless think that it should not be illegal. Again, prostitution comes to mind here; or gambling; or Morris dancing.

The point is that what you think of a practice is one thing, and what you think ought to be done about it in particular circumstances is another. Sometimes the two coincide, more often when your view of the practice is negative. Sometimes they do not, particularly in those cases which you think would be the beginning of a slippery slope, whereby at first similar, and then rather different, practices would come to be accepted which you think ought not to be. The distinction is especially important when it comes to the law. Opponents of abortion on demand might cite the 1967 UK Abortion Act as having come to licence in practice much more than the letter of that law; supporters might welcome it for just that reason, even if they think its conditions remain too narrow. People no less relaxed about gay than about straight sex might have welcomed the Homosexual Law Reform Act of 1962 in the expectation, which has turned out to be well founded, that despite the limitations of its legal provisions, it would lead to more homosexuality; clear-thinking homophobes – if that is not too absurd a thought – might have opposed it on those grounds (among others, of course).

Your moral view of a practice and of its being institutionalized, and in particular of its being legalized, are not one and the same. What you think about each of them can run in contrary directions. How do these considerations bear on the issue of legalizing what is morally wrong?

Legalizing what is morally wrong

Here again is the basic argument for legalizing interrogational torture. In certain circumstances torture is necessary, however regrettably: so the question is how best to limit it; and the best way of doing that is legally to restrict its use to just those circumstances. Furthermore, the twin advantages of legalization – getting information needed to avoid catastrophe without resorting to hypocrisy, and restricting torture to cases where it is necessary – outweigh its possibly negative consequences.

In respect of legalization and morality, the argument may be understood in two quite different ways. In light of what I have just outlined, it could be taken *either* as an argument in favour of legalizing something – interrogational torture – that is morally wrong; *or* as an argument that, since interrogational torture is in certain cases morally justifiable, it should be made legal. How, then, are we to understand the proposal to legalize interrogational torture? The issue is crucial. It is one thing to argue that, while of course torture, including interrogational torture, is morally repugnant, still, it should be legalized as "the lesser of two evils", if only to limit its use as far as possible. It is another to argue that interrogational torture, repugnant or not, is morally justifiable, even morally necessary. Posner's position, for instance, seems to be the latter. Dershowitz's, he himself insists, is the former. The issue takes us to the heart of the utilitarianism on which the advocates of legalizing interrogational torture rely: for while the distinction between the two positions is clear, utilitarianism in fact *rules out* the view that we ought to accept interrogational torture as "the lesser of two evils", morally repugnant though it is.

A useful way to make this clear, and to see why it matters so much, is to explore how Dershowitz takes his critics to task for wilfully misrepresenting him as a supporter of torture:

> In proposing some kind of advanced approval for the use of limited force in extreme situations, I deliberately declined to take a position on the normative issue of whether I would personally approve of the use of nonlethal torture against a captured terrorist who refuses to divulge

information deemed essential to prevent an avoidable act of mass terrorism, though I did set out the argument in favor of (and against) it. I sought a debate about a different, though related, issue: if torture would, [sic] *in fact* be employed by a democratic nation under the circumstances, would the rule of law and principles of accountability require that any use of torture be subject to some kind of judicial (or perhaps executive) oversight (or control)? On this normative issue, I have expressed my views loudly and clearly. My answer, unlike that of the Supreme Court of Israel, is yes. [4]

Regardless of his own view of torture, then, it appears that his view of its use by 'a democratic nation' is *either* that such a nation is justified in sometimes doing what is morally wrong (since torture is wrong); *or* that it is not justified in so doing (but that it will do so anyway); *or* that torture is not always morally wrong (since it is in certain cases, 'extremely rare' or otherwise, morally justified). So far, so good: his critics are mistaken if they assume that his position on legalizing interrogational torture *has* to be based on the third of these. That would be the case only if the first view – that it is sometimes right to do what is morally wrong, to choose the so-called lesser evil – were incoherent, as well as representing his own position; or that the second view was not his own, despite his later insistence that it is. This is what he says about what his position actually is:

> Let me once again present my actual views on torture, so that no one can any longer feign confusion about where I stand, though I'm certain that the "confusion" will persist among some who are determined to argue that I am a disciple of Torquemada.
>
> I am against torture as a *normative* matter, and I would like to see its use minimized. . . .
>
> I pose the issue as follows. If torture is, in fact, being used and/or would, in fact, be used in an actual ticking bomb terrorist case, would it be *normatively* better or worse to have such torture regulated by some kind of warrant, with accountability, recordkeeping, standards and limitations? This is an important debate, and a different one from the old, abstract Benthamite debate over whether torture can ever be justified. [5]

He insists that while he supports the legalization of torture, he is nonetheless morally opposed to it.

Now, we have already seen that it can make perfectly good sense to advocate legalizing something to which you are morally opposed. In the 1960s many people in the UK thought that homosexuality, or abortion, were morally wrong, but that nonetheless they should be made legal. That is an entirely coherent position. Even today, some anti-abortionists think it is better to keep abortion legal, because it is a good way – indeed, the only way – of limiting and controlling abortion. There is nothing incoherent about that. You can consistently oppose abortion (whether on utilitarian or on some other grounds) and at the same time think that the best practical way of opposing it is to legalize it (on utilitarian grounds). Or, as I suggested earlier, people morally opposed to the consumption of alcohol, cannabis or heroin might – and some do – think that legal prohibition is wrong because it leads to more, not less, consumption, and to the consumption of alcohol, cannabis and/or heroin which is tainted or impure, with consequences (even) worse than the consequences of the availability of these drugs. Dershowitz's stated position on torture seems to be just like this. He argues that a practice of which he morally disapproves should nonetheless be made legal, in order the better to control and limit it.

The trouble is, however, that it is impossible to read the fullest exposition of his position, in *Why Terrorism Works*, and seriously suppose that he does *not* think that interrogational torture is morally justified in ticking bomb cases, even though he does not say so explicitly. Take just a few examples. There is a section on 'the case for torturing the ticking bomb terrorist', [6] but no section on the case against. He says in that section, furthermore, that 'The simple cost-benefit analysis for employing such nonlethal torture seems overwhelming: it is surely better to inflict nonlethal pain on one guilty terrorist who is illegally withholding information needed to prevent an act of terrorism than to permit a large number of innocent victims to die.' [7] He goes on to argue that an act-utilitarian 'justification [of the use of interrogational torture] is simple-minded' because 'it has no inherent limiting principle', so that 'anything goes as long as the number of people tortured or killed does not exceed the number that would be saved'; and that we therefore need 'other constraints on what we can properly do', which 'can come from rule utilitarianisms or other principles of morality'. [8] Does that not imply that, with such constraints in place, interrogational torture is morally justifiable? And that what only 'seems overwhelming' in fact is overwhelming when qualified in this way? Now, I am not claiming that these (and other) passages *prove* that Dershowitz does indeed think interrogational torture is morally justifiable, but only that they make it inordinately difficult not to think he does. If (as for instance one reviewer of an earlier draft of this book insists) these passages are intended to offer, not his own view of interrogational torture, but the view of governmental officials – a view which, realistically, is unlikely to change – then it is unfortunate that he did not make this clear.

The difficulty is heightened, moreover, by the train driver example with which he opens his case and on which what follows in *Why Terrorism Works* relies. First, that example is designed to show that mowing down the drunk rather than the children is justified on account of its consequences; the relevant analogy is between mowing down the drunk and torturing the suspected terrorist on the one hand, and mowing down the children and letting the bomb go off on the other. It is not between mowing down the drunk and legalizing interrogational torture on the one hand, and mowing down the children and not legalizing interrogational torture on the other. Second, Dershowitz describes the train driver, and his students, as choosing the lesser evil in choosing to mow down the drunk. Again, in making an analogy between the train driver's situation and interrogational torture, it is hard to see how the notion of the lesser evil is intended in the text to apply to legalizing interrogational torture, rather than to interrogational torture itself. The impression to which that gives rise, furthermore, that Dershowitz thus thinks that interrogational torture is justifiable, is heightened by its being entirely reasonable for people to take 'evil', lesser or otherwise, as describing (interrogational) torture, rather than its legalization. And that impression is likely to be heightened still further by a certain difficulty in understanding what a utilitarian might mean by the notion of the lesser evil, as opposed to simply a good. Suppose your only choice really is to kill either two people or ten. Then you might describe killing two as the lesser evil, and mean by that simply that killing ten people is worse than killing two – even though killing two is morally wrong (paralleling Dershowitz's avowed opposition to interrogational torture). But that is *not* the utilitarian view. On a utilitarian view, there can be no such "tragic choices", but only choices among consequences; and that action which has the better, or the best, consequences is the one that is morally right. That is one reason why many people reject utilitarianism: in their view it cannot do justice to this element of our moral experience, the need sometimes to choose between different actions *all* of which really are morally problematic. For on a utilitarian view the action chosen – the one which leads to the least bad consequences – is the *right* one, just because it has those consequences. It is not "morally wrong but unfortunately necessary", but "morally right on account of its consequences". On a utilitarian view, then, Dershowitz's train driver does *not* have a choice between two moral wrongs. Her choice is between doing what is morally right and doing what is morally wrong – simply because that action is right which has the better (or the best) consequences. Any other action is simply *wrong*. There *can* be no action which is a "lesser evil": on a utilitarian view, an action like that is no evil at all, but simply the right thing to do.

There are two reasons, then, why critics of Dershowitz might perhaps be forgiven for supposing that he must be committed to the view that interrogational torture is morally justifiable, despite his insistence to the contrary. First, it is hard to see how the train driver example might be intended as offering an analogy with legalizing interrogational torture, rather than with torture itself. Second, the description of the train driver's choice in terms of the lesser evil is on a utilitarian view problematic; for on that view, lesser evils turn out in fact to be goods. Given the first difficulty, therefore, in light of which they already think Dershowitz must be talking about interrogational torture and not just its legalization, it seems unsurprising that critics should take him to be arguing that it is morally justified. Doubtless that impression is strengthened by the fact that he does not actually say, in *Why Terrorism Works*, that he thinks that interrogational torture should be legalized even though such torture is morally unjustifiable. Nor, when seeking to rectify that misinterpretation in his later comments, does he say what his reasons are for being 'against torture as a normative matter'.

The final factor which compounds this problem of the discrepancy between Dershowitz's own understanding of his position and most of his critics' understanding of it is his general interpretation of the utilitarianism on which he relies. His most detailed discussion of utilitarianism occurs in the course of his rejection of torturing people *other* than the detained suspected terrorist in order to obtain the information needed to avoid catastrophe:

The reason [Bentham's] kind of single-case utilitarian justification is simple-minded is that it has no inherent limiting principle. If non-lethal torture of one person is justified to prevent the killing of many important people, then what if it were necessary to use lethal torture – or at least torture that posed a substantial risk of death? What if it were necessary to torture the suspect's mother or children to get him to divulge the necessary information? What if it took threatening to kill his family, his friends, his entire village? Under a simple-minded quantitative case utilitarianism, anything goes as long as the number of people tortured or killed does not exceed the number that would be saved. This is morality by numbers, unless there are other constraints on what we can properly do. These other constraints can come from rule utilitarianisms or other principles of morality, such as the prohibition against deliberately punishing the innocent. Unless we are prepared to impose some limits on the use of torture or other barbaric tactics that might be of some use in preventing terrorism, we risk hurtling down a slippery slope into the abyss of amorality and ultimately tyranny. [9]

But, he continues: 'It does not necessarily follow from this understandable fear of the slippery slope that we can never consider the use of nonlethal infliction of pain, if its use were to be limited by acceptable principles of morality'. [10] People like Biletzki are mistaken in thinking that 'the "slippery slope" claim . . . when abetted by a utilitarian argument, leads to torture of not only the terrorist, but perhaps his wife, or his daughter, if so many lives are to be saved'. [11] Clearly, then, Dershowitz is concerned to avoid Bentham's 'simple-minded' utilitarianism because it suggests that 'a sufficiently large fear of catastrophe could conceivably authorize almost any plausibly efficacious government action'. [12]

The problem is this. What 'other principles of morality' *could* be consistently invoked to weigh against utilitarianism? Rule utilitarianism can of course be invoked as setting constraints on 'single-case', or act, utilitarianism: the harmful consequences for other cases of acting so as to bring about the best consequences in this case might well outweigh the latter. Consider sticking to the speed limit, not because of the consequences of breaking it in this case (a straight, deserted road, etc.) but because of the consequences for your own – or others' – inclination to stick to the speed limit in cases where it does matter, or your inclination in general to obey the law. And Dershowitz's position, as we have seen, is clearly rule utilitarian. But that is not to bring in 'other' principles of morality. Rule utilitarianism is still utilitarianism. If the consequences of 'threatening to kill his family, his friends, his entire village' could be somehow kept in check, so that they did not 'risk hurtling down a slippery slope into the abyss of amorality and ultimately tyranny', then rule utilitarianism would permit it. On a utilitarian view, innocence has no special status. Torturing, or killing, an innocent person is right or wrong solely according to the consequences of doing so. Not permitting *that* would therefore depend on empirical considerations concerning the likely consequences of such threats being used. The issue would be an empirical one – just as, on his rule utilitarian view, the rights and wrongs of Dershowitz's own proposal regarding legalizing interrogational torture of "guilty" suspects depend on an empirical evaluation of its likely consequences. The difficulty, however, is to see how non-utilitarian 'principles of morality' could be brought in. What could an 'inherent limiting principle' be, in the context of a utilitarian outlook? What sort of 'other constraints on what we can properly do' could utilitarianism allow? If torturing or killing innocents is wrong on *non-utilitarian* grounds, then why are other actions not wrong on similar, non-utilitarian, grounds – actions such as the interrogational torture of someone presumed "guilty" of planting a bomb? And on what grounds can one decide which actions are susceptible to utilitarian considerations and which are not? The point is that utilitarianism admits of no exceptions: either right and wrong is a matter of the consequences or it is not. To argue that something *justified on utilitarian grounds* can be 'limited by acceptable principles of morality' [13] which are not themselves utilitarian is nonsense. Nor is it enough simply to say, 'I agree', when commenting on a critic's argument that, if the ends justify the means, then torturing a suspect's child could be justified – but that 'The United States should not become such a nation'. [14] We need reasons for that conclusion, and we need to know whether or not they are non-utilitarian: for if they are, then they undermine the utilitarianism in terms of which Dershowitz makes his proposal.

Little wonder, then, that many critics should be confused by Dershowitz's insistence – in itself an entirely coherent position, whether or not you agree with it – that he opposes torture, while wanting to see it legalized. Nor, however, is it surprising that he should be genuinely piqued by the imputation that he supports torture, since he appears not to see that it is his presentation of his position, and to some extent also his misunderstanding of crucial aspects of it, which provokes that imputation. [15]

But it is not Dershowitz's grasp of utilitarianism or his use of the train driver example that really matter. What does matter is the substantive issue of legalizing interrogational torture and its likely consequences. In his unambiguous and unequivocal espousal of rule utilitarianism, he is in fact quite explicit about the central importance of institutional consequences and issues to do with the moral climate. His vigorous objections to invoking necessity after the event, on the grounds that necessity is a catch-all, make that clear. [16] Such a catch-all, he thinks, is morally corrosive, as is the hypocrisy of either ignoring torture or arguing that it should in certain cases be condoned, while remaining illegal. His brief consideration of objections to torture warrants is couched in just these terms:

> The major downside of any warrant procedure would be its legitimization of a horrible practice, but in my view it is better to legitimate and control a *specific* practice that will occur than to legitimate a *general* practice of tolerating extralegal actions so long as they operate under the table of scrutiny and beneath the radar screen of accountability. Judge Posner's "pragmatic" approach would be an invitation to widespread (and officially – if surreptitiously – approved) lawlessness in "extreme circumstances." Moreover, the very concept of "extreme circumstances" is subjective and infinitely expandable. [17]

So let us focus directly on the argument that institutionalizing interrogational torture would lead to a better moral state of affairs than the current hypocrisy of pretending that it does not happen.

Three Positive Claims about the Consequences of Legalizing Interrogational Torture

The first claim is that legalization would lead to fewer, not more, instances of torture: 'I believe, though I certainly cannot prove, that a formal requirement of a judicial warrant as a prerequisite to nonlethal torture would decrease the amount of physical violence directed against suspects.' [18] For while one might argue that 'if the courts authorize it [torture], it becomes a precedent', 'Tolerating an off-the-book system of secret torture can also establish a dangerous precedent'. [19] While admitting that it 'is always difficult to extrapolate from history', Dershowitz cites John Langbein's *Torture and the Law of Proof*, in which Langbein claims that 'when torture warrants were abolished, "the English experiment with torture left no traces". Because it was under centralized control, it was easier to abolish than in France, where it persisted for many years.' [20]

There are two difficulties here. First, how well-founded is the confidence that 'Requiring that decision [to torture] to be approved by a judicial officer will result in fewer instances of torture even if the judge rarely turns down a request' – not least on account of the admirably candid admission contained in the final clause? [21] I certainly cannot share that confidence. Nor does it take account of the commonplace experience of interrogators and torturers going beyond what is sanctioned, whether tacitly or otherwise. In the wake of the Landau Commission, for instance, which had sanctioned torture without formally legalizing it, 'it was common for the GSS interrogators to knowingly go beyond the directives set by the Landau Commission Report and the ministerial committee, both in using methods which exceeded the limits set in these directives and then lying about it'. [22] It is surely incumbent on advocates of legalizing interrogational torture to offer something more solid than brief speculation as evidence that formal legalization would work in the opposite direction. Of course one 'cannot prove' it; but that is pretty disingenuous. What is needed is not *proof*, but reasonably sound *evidence*. That is all the more so because people who actually have experience of the realities of torture remain convinced that, while the 'semi-formal status of torture *supposedly* protects it from corruption and from deterioration to a more "barbaric" form', [23] it in fact does nothing of the sort. Certainly, such detailed evidence as we have, as opposed to anecdote and hearsay, supports this view. B'Tselem, the Israeli Information Centre for Human Rights in the Occupied Territories, makes that plain in its 2000 position paper on legalizing interrogational torture. Addressing 'the social, moral, and political consequences that would result from such legislation', [24] it concludes, on the basis of some forty pages of evidence, that it is only 'by tenaciously clinging to the absolute prohibition on any form of physical force' [25] (which in the paper's context means torture) that the incidence of torture can be prevented from spreading even further than it already has.

Optimism on this score is unfounded. Nor does looking at history do anything to dispel this scepticism. The argument Dershowitz offers, that, since legalizing torture hastened its abolition, we too should legalize it, is hardly convincing. [26] If legalizing torture had hastened its abolition, there would have been no torture left, later to make illegal (and, still later, to legalize).

The second difficulty is the assumption that 'most [most!] judges would require compelling evidence' and 'law enforcement officials would be reluctant to seek a warrant unless they had compelling evidence that the suspect had information needed to prevent an imminent terrorist attack'; so that in fact 'the rights of the suspect would be better protected with a warrant requirement'. [27] Thus the duly acknowledged danger – that, since the 'suspected terrorist we may choose to torture is a "they" – an enemy with whom we do not identify . . . [there is a] risk of making the wrong decision, or of overdoing the torture . . . ' [28] – would be diminished. But again, how realistic is such optimism? To judge by the efforts that both the US and the UK governments continue to make to ensure judicial compliance with their "new realism" – the 2001 Patriot Act and Guantanamo Bay in the USA, the 2005 Prevention of Terrorism Act in the UK – pessimism seems much more clearly indicated. The fact that judges would have to be persuaded that the alleged danger was imminent would have two consequences. First, it would lead the intelligence services to do their very best to persuade them; and, second, it would lead judges themselves to seek to avoid the risk of "getting it wrong" in refusing the warrant (which, as we have seen, Dershowitz himself admits). It would take a brave judge to risk the imminent disaster by not granting a warrant to torture in a particular case, when it had been agreed that such torture was in the right circumstances legally justified. Of course, my prognostications are not based on very much firmer evidence than others' to the contrary; and of course I hope that the evidence necessary to settle the issue will remain unavailable. Still, such evidence as there is around the world of professionals' compliance with torture suggests that the "realists'" optimism is hardly well-founded. How long would torture remain a last resort, whether in the minds of the judiciary, the secret services, the government or indeed people at large? The Twinings' scepticism seems to me more realistic than any "realism":

Even an out-and-out utilitarian can support an absolute prohibition against institutionalized torture on the ground that no government in the world can be trusted not to abuse the power and to satisfy in practice the conditions he [Bentham] would impose. [29]

The second positive claim is that legalization would eliminate the present resort to "necessity" as a retrospective excuse for breaking the law. I agree that 'No legal system operating under the rule of law should ever tolerate an "off-the-books" approach to necessity', since 'The road to tyranny has always been paved with claims of necessity made by those responsible for the security of a nation'. [30] But I am not so sanguine that the judiciary would just obviously be a better safeguard against such claims than the politicians, not least because, as I suggested above, the pressure on the judiciary under the torture warrant proposal would be so much greater than it is now. Legalizing interrogational torture, even in the narrowest of circumstances, would radically alter the moral climate within which (among other things) the judiciary would be operating. As Langbein recounts (and Dershowitz himself acknowledges) it was precisely the judiciary who authorized torture in the past: so why should we expect its legalization, and thus its judicial control, not to lead to the very expansion of torture that he opposes, rather than to its diminution? Far from serving as a defence, at least in principle, against 'claims of necessity made by those responsible for the security of a nation', the judiciary would be drawn into precisely *that* responsibility. The confidence that it is just plain obvious that it is worse that 'the decision to torture a ticking bomb terrorist . . . be relegated to a local policeman, FBI agent, or CIA operative, rather than to a judge, the attorney general, or the president' [31] is at best too quick, and at worst disconcerting.

The third claim is that it would eliminate the present hypocritical pretence that "we" do not torture. But the institutional damage done by deceit and hypocrisy can be prevented *either* by admitting that "we" torture *or* by ceasing to torture. Which choice is preferable depends on the independent grounds that there are for judging it morally justifiable or not. To say that a practice cannot be eradicated does not constitute an argument, or even the slightest evidence, that it is *morally justifiable.* The best it could do (if at least probably correct) would be to suggest that the issue of legality needs to be considered in terms of whether legalization would or would not lead to less institutional harm than that caused by prohibition; and that returns us to the substantive argument. It is important to be clear about this, so let us briefly consider an analogous example. [32] The Dutch and the Swedish governments both agree that, while prostitution is morally at least questionable (for all sorts of reasons, and whether rightly or wrongly), simple legal prohibition is impractical. But while the Dutch have therefore legalized both the sale and the purchase of sexual services, in Sweden their sale is legal but their purchase is not. That is to say, the Swedish government is trying to stop demand rather than supply, because it thinks that it is the demand that is morally problematic. The Dutch, while agreeing with that, think that a legal ban would not work. The point is that even if the Dutch are right about that, it does not show that their moral qualms about buying and selling sex are not genuine. Ironically, Dershowitz's insistence that his advocacy of the legalization of interrogational torture does not commit him to the view that torture is morally justifiable, however problematic, suggests that he understands that distinction quite clearly. [33] But then his arguments for legalizing interrogational torture rest only on the assumption that abolition is simply unrealistic, that a "Swedish solution" is not available, and that therefore only a "Dutch solution" remains. Moreover, the little he actually does say about the likely impact of his proposal on the moral climate is unconvincing. Abolition may indeed be unrealistic as things currently stand in the USA and the UK. Nonetheless, both countries *could* end the present hypocrisy simply by stopping torture altogether, whether by their own intelligence services and troops, or via the obscenity of "rendition".

To sum up. Despite the extraordinarily serious nature of their policy proposal, advocates of legalizing interrogational torture say very little about the likely consequences of its institutionalization. Even Dershowitz, who says more than anyone else, barely touches the surface. Yet the likely impact of the normalization of torture on the moral climate is critical. And such evidence as we already have of the impact of its normalization – whether via the hypocritical route of actually existing practice or via the hardly less hypocritical route of quasi-legalization – points to its likely spread, not to its control and limitation. Writing of Pierre Vidal-Naquet's analysis of the Algerian experience, Edward Peters reports that Vidal-Naquet was convinced that 'The cancer was not the torture itself, but the public indifference to it that eroded and rendered meaningless even the most explicit protections afforded by civil rights and public law'. [34] No one offers any argument why legal acceptance of interrogational torture should not increase public indifference, rather than galvanizing public abhorrence of its wider spread. Seth Kreimer's summary here is particularly apt:

> Professor Dershowitz asserts that 'sometimes' torture will be ineluctably necessary; the converse of this assertion is that 'sometimes' torture will wreak human havoc without any discernable, much less proportionate public benefit, and 'sometimes' the benefits sought could be achieved without torture. It is far from clear that an institutional structure that contemplates 'torture warrants' would minimize those latter 'times'. Indeed, under current circumstances, such an institution is likely to encourage officials to yield to . . . the 'mortal temptation of instantaneous efficacity'. [35]

The Institutionalization of Interrogational Torture

There are no good grounds to suppose that the consequences of formal legalization would not be a further extension of torture, rather than its eradication. By contrast, there are good grounds to think that it would be a step – or more likely, a leap – on a slippery slope towards a torturous society. 'What was to be done "just once"', to quote Amnesty International, 'will become an institutionalized practice and will erode the moral and legal principles that stand against a form of violence that could affect all of society'. [36] 'As a basis for public policy regarding interrogation methods', therefore, the proposal to legalize it 'is disastrous, serving only to rationalize the institutionalization of torture'. [37]

I shall group further reasons for this conclusion under four heads: (1) its impact on the use of torture; (2) its legal impact; (3) its impact on potential terrorist bombers; and (4) the professionalization of torture. (Inevitably, though, there will be a little overlap, both with previous comments and with each other.)

The impact of legalization on the use of torture

If utilitarian considerations justify torturing the "guilty terrorist", then how do they fail to justify torturing *several* detainees, *any one* of whom might well know the whereabouts of the bomb? After all, as we saw in chapter two, the ticking bomb scenario is characterized not by certainty, but only by probability. So why not go further, and if necessary torture the families and friends of suspects? This is not just an academic question about the implications of utilitarianism as a moral theory. If such a use of torture once led to a bomb before it went off, then it would be difficult for interrogators to resist the temptation to resort to torturing, say, a suspect's mother on a future occasion when the suspect remained impervious, and the clock was continuing to tick. After all, and again as we saw earlier, Dershowitz himself tells us that 'Jordan apparently broke the most notorious terrorist of the 1980s, Abu Nidal, *by threatening his mother*'. [38] There might even be a deterrent effect on potential bomb-planters if they knew that their mother, father, children and/or associates might be tortured to try to stop it going off. And as a result of that, it would also become increasingly tempting for people to think that such "third party" torture was morally justifiable; and for lawyers to propose that the scope of torture warrants should be extended to legalize that practice.

Furthermore, why limit torture to "known" cases of ticking bombs? Suppose the intelligence services suspect that some people are planning to do something soon that might well be catastrophic. Ordinary interrogation has not succeeded in extracting the information needed. Why not torture them, just in case their suspicions are justified? Or suppose they suspect that someone they have arrested knows of such a plan, to be implemented by others, and whose identity the captive either knows, or might perhaps know. Again, ordinary interrogation has not succeeded in extracting the information needed: why not torture them, just in case their suspicions are justified, just in case there is a ticking bomb? The less imminent the possible catastrophe, after all, the greater the chances that torture would extract the information needed to prevent the catastrophe. If torture sometimes works, why not torture as a matter of routine, just in case someone knows something that might turn out to be useful? For as Jeremy Waldron insists about the torture at Abu Ghraib, it 'had nothing to do with "ticking bomb" terrorism. It was intended to "soften up" detainees so that US military intelligence could get information from them about likely attacks by Iraqi insurgents against American occupiers.' [39] How confident should we be that that sort of thinking, and the torture that follows from it, would not be encouraged by legalizing interrogational torture?

In short, why not extend interrogational torture beyond just those circumstances where, since time is most pressing, it is least likely to
succeed? Why not use it, as other interrogational methods are used, to
pre-empt ticking bombs? After all, surely pre-empting ticking bombs
is preferable to dealing with them. Given the central role of pre-emptive
attacks in the "war on terror", surely pre-emption is no less to the point
here? [40]

Why not go even further, and consider the use of intimidatory
torture as a means of seriously putting people off joining terrorist
organizations, and/or becoming potential bomb-planters, in the first
place? If torture sometimes works as a means of getting information,
as its advocates claim it does, why would it not work just as well as an
intimidatory tool? It has often enough been used to intimidate people,
and with all too much success (though with "counter-productive"
consequences as well): consider Nazi-occupied Europe, Chile under
Pinochet, Greece under the Colonels, China, Guatemala, El Salvador,
Honduras and, more recently, Burma, Sierra Leone, Liberia, Zimbabwe
and Iraq, to name just a few. [41] Of course, it is the case that 'it appears
that the implicit assumption of most of the people who consider ticking
bomb examples is that the interrogee is, in some way, responsible for
the creation of the danger itself'. [42] The advocates both of legalizing
interrogational torture and of non-legal interrogational torture all
assume or insist that the interrogators know that their captive knows
where the bomb is (however implausibly, as we saw in the previous
chapter). But why limit it to the allegedly guilty terrorist, if it is *the
consequences alone* which justify or fail to justify an action?

Nor is that all. As a first-year student pointed out to me in discussion, how do proponents of interrogational torture propose to deal
with children who might be trained to plant bombs? [43] Are they
"innocent" on account of their age? Or "guilty" on account of what
they have "done", whether or not they can tell right from wrong? Either
way, on utilitarian grounds, why not torture them to prevent the
catastrophe?

Advocates of legalizing interrogational torture owe us an answer to
all these questions.

Nor should we be sanguine that legalizing interrogational torture
would limit its use to alleged cases of terrorism. Once torture were
normalized in so-called ticking bomb cases, once it had been made
legally thinkable, what reasons are there to suppose its use would not

spread to other sorts of circumstance? The *Economist* – hardly a left-leaning publication – certainly thinks it would:

> How will the counterterrorist program uphold a monopoly on the use of torture? Investigators of many other crimes – narcotics trafficking, serial murder, sabotage of information systems, espionage, financial scams – will consider their own pursuits compelling. . . . Both US and British judiciaries have struggled for decades with the overwhelming ill consequences of coercive interrogation of suspects. [44]

And the *Economist* appears to be right. Dershowitz was recently invoked by name by the police and lawyers in the USA in *quite different* circumstances from those he himself is concerned with:

> The brief for the petitioner, seeking to exonerate the police officer who persisted in questioning the wounded and screaming suspect, invoked the image of an official questioning a 'suspect [who] has been arrested for kidnaping [*sic*] a small child who cannot survive without immediate adult intervention. The child is being hidden somewhere, and time is running out on his life,' and invited the Court to refer to Professor Dershowitz's analysis. [45]

If the survival of the thousands of people whose lives are at stake if the bomb goes off justifies torture, as legalizing it would be very widely taken to imply, whether or not that was the view of those who had advocated its legalization, then why not the survival of all those whose lives are threatened, say, by drugs? After all, the seriousness of "the war on terrorism" is matched only by that of "the war on drugs", just as it was matched in the past by "the war against 'the Evil Empire'".

As for empirical evidence of what happens when torture is not absolutely ruled out, one need look no further than the B'Tselem paper already cited [46] and Human Rights Watch's 1992 report on Israel, the late twentieth-century testing ground no less for systematic interrogational torture than for Dershowitz's thinking about it. [47] The point – and it is a pretty obvious one, even if apparently not to a whole swathe of academics and lawyers – is this:

> Torture, like power, appears to be habit-forming. The rationale of torture in an age of terror – averting imminent and massive harm to civilians by torturing the right source – easily slides to cover ever more

remote sources and more hypothetical harms. It is difficult to torture just a little. [48]

In the aftermath of the 1987 Landau Commission, torture became quasi-legal. Although it remained *formally* illegal, the explicit recognition of the retrospective defence of "necessity" meant that it was *de facto* legally permitted. Torturers were deemed to have acted illegally, but, in retrospect, justifiably. Hypocritical or not, the result of such legal sanction after the event was an increasing use of torture. [49] Why should the need to obtain permission have a directly contrary effect to knowing that, in effect, permission would be granted retrospectively? We are not told. However, what we do know is this. In Israel,

> human rights organizations and their lawyers have unearthed the abusive and opportunistic use made of the ticking time-bomb argument by the security services in order to obtain permission to torture in cases that are far removed from any kind of an immediate-danger scenario. The evidence amassed in the hundreds of suits and depositions points clearly to a cheapening of the ticking time-bomb rationale. [50]

Why think that things would be different anywhere else?

Certainly, the increasing unofficial sanctioning of torture worldwide since the First World War is one factor in its undisputed spread. Legal warrants would counter precisely this, it is claimed. But to repeat: why should officially sanctioning torture, legalizing it, lead to less torture when unofficially sanctioning it does the opposite? Of course, the question is an empirical one. It cannot be settled other than by the sort of "experiment" that instantiating such a proposal would in fact be. But such evidence as there is of legalizing practices hitherto illegal suggests that the practices concerned tend to expand, rather than to diminish. [51] To the extent that counterfactual argument has a place here, furthermore, the idea that legalizing interrogational torture in ticking bomb situations would make for less torture is wildly implausible. Again, consider the use of torture in the 1970s in Pinochet's Chile or the Colonels' Greece: how likely is it that legalizing interrogational torture in the extreme would have helped to reduce its wider and/or "unofficial" incidence? [52] Democracies are different though, the advocates of interrogational torture assume. Maybe so, maybe not. But if so, then what of the UK? What reason is there to think that there would have been less torture in Northern Ireland in the 1970s if the UK had legalized its interrogational use in ticking bomb situations? None has been suggested to support such a dubious proposition.

In summary, there are three interrelated reasons why I think that legalizing torture would be likely to lead to other people than "guilty terrorists" alone being tortured. First, there is the practical likelihood of interrogators taking it as a "green light". Second, the utilitarian reasoning employed to attempt to justify the proposal would, if successful, sanction torturing people who *might* know where the bomb was, and also people who clearly *did not know* but whose torture would put pressure on someone thought to know where it was. Third, it would be a "green light" not only for interrogators, but also for politicians and academics, even further to extend the torture that is already going on. As a soldier in the then Rhodesia put it, 'When you do it [torture], you are in that condition of "conscience-narrowing" and strangely obsessed to get information. So you inflict pain, maim and kill to get what you want.' [53] The observation applies no less to politicians and academics than to soldiers or interrogators. In short, a likely outcome of legalizing interrogational torture is the normalization of torture.

The impact of legalizing interrogational torture on the law

What would be the worldwide legal impact of the United States' – or indeed the United Kingdom's – legalizing torture? Certainly, 'Were the United States . . . to declare its intention to allow nonlethal torture in the ticking bomb case, that declaration would effectively change international law, since our actions help define the law.' Admirably "realistic" though Dershowitz's own judgement is, however, the only comment he offers on it is that 'the stakes are far higher in the debate now taking place in this country [than in Israel]'. [54] But it is obvious that if the paragon of democracy that is the United States legalized torture, the incentive for others to follow suit would be enormous: just imagine the media headlines in whichever you consider to be the most vicious of today's many dictatorships. It is inconceivable that non-democratic governments would not take their cue from the legalization of interrogational torture by "democracies". And why stop there? Why not rescind other central pillars of international law, such as the Geneva Convention? The USA's cavalier approach to that 'quaint' [55] pillar of international law, in keeping with its wider disregard in that area, may look like an assertion of American untouchability to those unable to see themselves as others do. As a contribution to securing democratic values around the world it is, however, counterproductive – to say the least. Legalizing interrogational torture would further encourage not only America's flight from the moral high ground, but would serve also to encourage others to follow suit. Already some of the loudest voices raised in the USA against the Bush administration's various attempts to justify the use of torture by other names, furthermore, come from military figures worried about the consequences for "their own", for captured American troops. Their "realism" is surely also to the point. The likelihood has to be that torture around the world would increase, if only on account of the example set.

Coming back to home, how confident can we be that the judiciary would always stick to the spirit as well as the letter of the rules? It seems unlikely. Not only would judges be pressured into issuing torture warrants for fear of failing to have prevented an allegedly preventable catastrophe, as I have already argued, but they would also become increasingly reliant 'on the showings made by the officials who seek the warrants'. [56] Recall how the US and UK secret services' "information" was "embellished" in the run-up to the 2003 invasion of Iraq. That is more than enough to show how dangerous it is simply to rely on "intelligence information". And even if "undoctored", we know as a result of the many failures of "intelligence" – from 11 September 2001 in the USA to 7 July 2005 in the UK – that the quality of such information is nowhere near reliable enough to avoid mistakes. So how many cases of torturing suspects who turned out to be innocent would be too many? How would the judges concerned react to news that they had authorized the torture of an innocent person? Would they resign in horror? Or, like the academic advocates of legalizing torture, would they too think the price worth paying? And what would be the impact of that on people's respect for the law? Of course, any system of criminal justice is likely sometimes wrongly to convict an innocent person. But torture is not to be compared even with wrongful imprisonment, dreadful though that is (as I argue in chapter four).

How precisely, furthermore, would the rules be specified? If only for fear of letting the one ticking bomb terrorist slip through the net, it is overwhelmingly likely that 'the resulting standards would inevitably be over-inclusive, resulting in unnecessary torture'. [57] On top of that, what would be the likely impact on the rest of the judiciary of some of its own members' officiating in torture in this way – especially if direct oversight of the conditions governing warrants were deemed desirable, or even necessary, as indeed Peters reminds us was in fact the case when torture was legal in most of Europe? [58] As David Luban reminds us, the vast majority of 'Judges do not fight their culture – they reflect it'. [59] What would be the impact of the legal acceptance of interrogational torture on judicial attitudes in other areas of the criminal law? I am pessimistic: but again, the question is not even addressed.

It seems to me, in fact, that the judicial "spread" of torture to which its legalization might be expected to lead is aptly illustrated by the way in which the legal "opinions" offered by leading academic lawyers around the Bush administration was itself a factor in Afghanistan, Guantanamo, Abu Ghraib and beyond. These lawyers, in their notorious attempts to "redefine" both torture and the scope of the Geneva Convention, [60] 'illustrate as graphically as any group how quickly and easily a secret culture of torture supporters can emerge even in the heart of a liberal culture'. [61] Just as, once torture comes to be discussed as a legitimate policy tool, it will come to be used in practice, so, once torture comes to be recognized as a legitimate legal tool, its legalized use will spread.

And there is more. "Administrative issues" would inevitably arise, and there would have to be ways of resolving them. Who exactly is entitled to ask whom for a torture warrant, and for precisely how long? Just how pressing must circumstances be believed to be to allow exactly what exceptions? These problems would also be more likely to serve to increase torture rather than diminish it. As Parry and White point out (in the American context),

> Congress would have to craft legislative standards for when and how to torture (e.g., how long can interrogators hold someone's head under water?), delegate that task to the executive, or entrust the torture decision to executive branch discretion. If the executive branch drafted regulations, the courts would engage in review to make sure the executive's interpretations were reasonable and within the range of permitted activity, and would preside over any subsequent cases. All three branches would thus play a role in creating the framework for torture,

and all three branches would become complicit in it. Finally, no matter how carefully the respective branches performed their appointed tasks, the resulting standards would inevitably be over-inclusive, resulting in unnecessary torture. [62]

Again, the evidence there is of how "professional standards" or "professional ethics" operate hardly inspires confidence. Both judiciary and politicians (let alone others) in Nazi Germany, in Argentina under military dictatorship, in the ex-Soviet Union – to name but a very few – increasingly sacrificed such of their scruples as remained for "the greater good", as what was once unthinkable came to be normalized.

Turning to the interrogators themselves, they would come under enormous pressure to apply for a warrant, "just in case": a

professional investigator – a person who owes a duty to the public to investigate the possibility of future terrorist activities – may not feel that she can ignore the availability of a torture warrant. If the investigator thinks that a court . . . will grant her application for a torture warrant, she will experience enormous pressure to apply for such a warrant. . . . If the court grants the application, the investigator will again experience enormous pressure to act on that warrant. [63]

The line having been drawn beyond, rather than before, interrogational torture, torturers will also be quicker to go beyond it. As Kreimer observes, 'If torture is permitted with a warrant, it will become increasingly difficult to refrain from torture without one'. [64] Nor is this simply a matter of unsubstantiated pessimism or optimism about how people are likely to behave. Such empirical evidence as there is, again from Israel, favours pessimism: 'To legalize is to encourage. Israel tried to limit use of physical coercion to extreme cases, but its security forces have ended up using such methods far more widely than was initially foreseen.' [65] Anat Biletzki confirms the *Economist*'s view:

During this past decade [c. 1990–2000], the High Court has heard hundreds of appeals by Palestinian detainees complaining of physical and psychological methods of "pressure". The court has often issued orders nisi and interim injunctions against these measures. Still, when the State has appealed against such injunctions, the court has almost invariably accepted the ticking time-bomb argument, citing security as its overriding concern. In almost all cases in which the court was petitioned to intervene and put a stop to inhuman treatment, and in which the state, i.e., the security forces, demanded continuance, the court shied away from taking a firm stand for human rights, claiming either unjusticiability or permitting the atrocities to continue as "necessary". [66]

As things currently stand, furthermore, state functionaries can refuse to torture because it is illegal. That defence would no longer be available. And that is no small matter. As Mark Danner points out, 'interrogation methods officially intended for use only on prisoners not protected by the Geneva Convention, like those in Guantanamo, "migrate" . . . and are employed on prisoners in Iraq who are entitled to such protection'. [67] This is why Posner opposes the legalization of torture, whether hypocritically or otherwise, for all his insistence that 'if the stakes are high enough, torture is permissible' and that 'No one who doubts that should be in a position of responsibility'. [68] For, he argues, 'If legal rules are promulgated permitting torture in defined circumstances, officials are bound to want to explore the outer bounds of the rules; and the practice, once it were thus regularized, would be likely to become regular'. [69] The very notion of respect for the law would come under enormous pressure – to be replaced by increasing contempt for it, and a contempt that would be justified. If *torture* is legal, so much the worse for the law. Jeremy Waldron makes the point decisively:

> The prohibition on torture is expressive of an important underlying policy of the law, which we might try to capture in the following way: Law is not brutal in its operation. Law is not savage. Law does not rule through abject fear and terror, or by breaking the will of those whom it confronts. If law is forceful or coercive, it gets its way by nonbrutal methods which respect rather than mutilate the dignity and agency of those who are its subjects. . . .
>
> For example, when a defendant charged with a serious offense is brought into a courtroom, he is brought in whether he likes it or not; and when he is punished, he is subject to penalties that are definitely unwelcome and that he would avoid if he could. In these instances, there is no doubt that he is subject to force, that he is coerced. But in these cases force and coercion do not work by reducing him to a quivering mass of 'bestial, desperate terror', the aim of every torturer. [70]

In all these interrelated ways, the consequences of legalizing interrogational torture would be to corrupt the very idea of law. Not only would it lead to an extension of the use of torture; it would also lead to a diminution of the respect for the law which – among other things – is a necessary condition of its even potentially regulating and limiting torture. Perhaps it is not surprising, then – however intellectually reprehensible – that no advocate of legalizing interrogational torture has to my knowledge published any sort of proposed draft of the legislation they have in mind.

The impact of legalization on potential bombers

It is worth reflecting on how potential "terrorists" might react to the legalization of interrogational torture. Are there likely to be more or fewer "ticking bombs"? I can do no more than speculate, but it seems to me at least as plausible to suppose that the "martyrdom to torture" of a member or members of a terrorist organization would lead to more, rather than to fewer, volunteers. What we know of volunteers for so-called suicide bombing certainly suggests that many feel themselves compelled to go to such an extreme fundamentally on account of what they perceive (rightly or wrongly) as the enormity of what the target regime has done. Hany Abu-Assad's 2005 film, *Paradise Now*, makes the point quite brilliantly. [71] Those responsible for the London bombings of July 2005, for instance, cited the UK government's role in the bombing and occupation of Iraq, with its attendant atrocities, as their motivation. In terms of "terrorism", then, legalizing interrogational torture is likely to lead to renewed determination.

Not only that: it would also in all likelihood lead to more, rather than less, sympathy for all sorts of terrorist causes. For again, no country – and certainly not the USA, or even the UK – that had legalized torture could lay claim to the moral high ground. The brutality of the "terrorist" would have been replicated by the state. It is no surprise that none of the regimes that routinely torture "terrorists" – Jordan and Egypt, for example – appear greatly to have deterred "terrorism". Nor do "terrorists" appear to have suffered any loss of morale as a result of the state's resorting to torture. One cost, then, of implementing the proposal to legalize interrogational torture might well be more, not fewer, actual bombings. David Rose reports the following statement from a 'senior Pentagon intelligence analyst': 'Quite frankly I'd have thought that if they weren't terrorists before they went to Gitmo [Guantanamo Bay], they would have been by the time they came out.' [72] You can see what they meant; and interrogational torture is likely to have the same effect as Guantanamo Bay, on potential sympathizers if not on the actual people tortured. Nor is that just my own view. Even the British Secretary of State for Foreign Affairs, Margaret Beckett, has 'warned that the camp was as much a "radicalizing and destabilizing influence" as it was an aid in the "war on terror"'. [73] I am not claiming, of course, that this would be bound to happen, but only that, at the very least, the view that it would is far more plausible than the contrary.

The impact of legalization on the professionalization of torture

The 'torturer is doing a *job*, he [or she] is "doing torture"; ... he [or she] is supposed to do it well, "mastering torture"'. [74] I argued in the previous chapter that legalizing interrogational torture would require the recognition of torture as a profession. That, you might think, is objection enough: what sort of society is it which regards the profession of torturer as a key public service? Still, many western societies in fact do just that, while pretending not to. To respond adequately to that reality, we need to be realistic about what it would be to make an explicitly *recognized* profession of torture.

As Ronald Crelinsten graphically details, the profession of torturer – in common with other professions – develops an internal dynamic. It seeks to expand its own scope, protect its members and so on: 'the very process of routinization of torture involves a kind of continuous and dynamic distortion of facts and events which, in the end, amounts to the construction of a new reality'. [75] The inculcation of obedience to authority, the creation of "enemies", the need to achieve "results" to justify resources, leading to finding ever more such "enemies" and the expansion of what counts as information all lead to the creation of a particular social reality. And 'This socially constructed reality – the routine of torture – replaces objective reality with one that is presumed to exist. In doing so, it also supplants conventional morality, substituting in its place the ideological dictates of the authority structure within which torture occurs.' [76] Think of Turkey, Colombia and more recently Afghanistan, Guantanamo Bay and Iraq. Or as Amnesty

International puts it, 'those who torture once will go on using it, encouraged by its "efficiency" in obtaining the confession or information they seek, whatever the quality of those statements. They will argue within the security apparatus for the extension of torture . . . they may form elite groups of interrogators to refine its practice.' [77] Legally legitimating the profession of torturer would not only give the practice itself an enormous impetus, but radically reconfigure people's conceptions of everyday decency. Slavoj Žižek has rightly pointed out that "ticking bomb" thinking is already corrupting the everyday culture of the United States, where 'The problem for those in power is how to get people to do the dirty work without turning them into monsters'. [78] In short, what a Brazilian torturer is reported to have told a prisoner would cease to appear bizarre: 'I'm a serious professional. After the revolution, I will be at your disposal to torture whom you like.' [79]

But it does not stop there. What about the training required for the profession of torturer? Institutionalizing interrogational torture requires that "we" ask people to be trained, and ask others to train them, to act in ways in which "we" ourselves would not be willing to act. Again, Crelinsten offers a summary of what is required. [80] On whom should trainee torturers practise? On whom should their trainers practise? How can "we" justify asking others to undergo the necessary abuse, humiliation, and elimination of moral sensibility? How can "we" ask people to go to, and to give, 'Special classes . . . where new torturers are shown what torture looks like, either in filmed demonstrations or even live demonstrations on actual prisoners', [81] or on colleagues or on people "picked up" from the streets? [82] Consider the case of 'Specialist Sean Baker, a former Gitmo military policeman and guard, who was discharged from the US Army because of injuries he sustained while pretending to be a prisoner': 'the Army's Physical Evaluation Board stated' that his traumatic brain injury was due to his 'playing the role of detainee who was non-cooperative and was being extracted from a detention cell in Guantanamo Bay, Cuba, during a training exercise'. [83] Yet that is what legalization demands. Of course, Dershowitz is quite right that thinking about legalization exposes our hypocrisy, since the profession of torturer already exists. To legalize its existence, however, rather than legislating for its prohibition, is altogether something else. To admit the profession of torturer to the range of legally recognized professions would require that we recognize torture training in the same way that we recognize, for example, legal, medical and teacher education and training – as John Gray reminds us in his splendidly titled Swiftian satire, 'A modest proposal: for preventing torturers in liberal democracies from being abused, and for recognizing their benefit to the public'. [84] And that is something that surely needs to be weighed in the balance, both in respect of institutionalizing the profession of torturer and of the further consequences that would follow from that.

Nor are torturers the only professionals who would require appropriate training. The necessary role of medical personnel is well documented. Writing of the period 1250–1750, Peters reminds us that – just as Dershowitz proposes – 'The torture itself was surrounded by protocols: it could not be savage or cause death or permanent injury . . . ; a medical expert had to be present; and a notary had to make an official record of the procedure.' [85] He goes on to remind us that medical complicity in torture reached its apogee under the Nazis: 'not only did the Third Reich bring back torture, but it transformed it into a medical speciality, a transformation which was to have great consequences in the second half of the twentieth century'. [86] Little if any research has been carried out on the impact on doctor–patient relations of the medical profession of a country's being associated (in fact if not in law) with torture, but it is hardly controversial to suppose that it is unlikely to be conducive to trust. The objections of Israel's Physicians for Human Rights to a situation where, for example, 'all active GSS interrogation centers are staffed by physicians 24 hours a day' [87] is in part testament to exactly the corrosion of values we might expect. Or consider the conclusions of two doctors reflecting on 'actual practice at Guantanamo', where both 'behavioral science consultants and others who are responsible for crafting and carrying out interrogation strategies' [88] and the interrogators themselves had access to medical records in order to help tailor torture techniques to the physical and mental states and capacities of individual prisoners: 'Wholesale disregard for clinical confidentiality is a large leap across the threshold, since it makes every caregiver into an accessory to intelligence gathering.' [89] What would that do to the profession of medicine?

All the professional medical bodies which insist that their members do not "assist" in torture (for all that this is all too often ignored) would presumably have to withdraw that instruction. Torture would now be a legally permitted activity, making medical cooperation, advice and training in interrogational torture on a par with the provision of medical services in prisons. [90] It is one thing to offer professional medical expertise in the context, say, of trying to rehabilitate sex offenders; it is entirely another to complete 'fitness evaluation forms' [91] which certify the degree and type of torture to which an individual may in their opinion be subjected without "undue" danger of death. How would that affect the ethics of health care? What would it do to the very idea of being a doctor or a nurse?

Perhaps doctors and researchers would be permitted a conscience clause on the basis of which they would not need to take part, whether indirectly or directly. [92] But on what grounds? Given the necessity of interrogational torture to avoid imminent catastrophe – a necessity that would now be legally recognized – such an exercise of conscience seems hardly justified, at least on the utilitarian grounds assumed by proponents of the idea. Certainly, if the services of a sufficient number were to be obtained, then the more medical professionals refused to take part, the greater the need not to allow a conscience clause. The "realism" of the advocates of legalizing interrogational torture means that they must be committed to the view, whether they are actually aware of it or not, that a doctor's responsibility is not always to their patient, but is at least in some circumstances to society as a whole (whether or not to the state). So why make an exception here? After all, it would be likely to lead to exceptions elsewhere. Well, which exceptions; and where? Once again, those who call for the legalization of interrogational torture are being almost unbelievably irresponsible in simply ignoring these issues. It is one thing to argue that doctors, nurses and other health professionals have responsibilities which go wider than individual patients (consider immunization, isolation and other public health issues) and quite another to license such professionals to treat individuals not as persons, but as bodies. And that is precisely what torture is. As Hadas Ziv puts it, 'The bureaucratization of a medical task . . . makes it possible to reduce the treatment process to a purely technical one – directed at the body, not the person'. [93] If it is legally permitted – or indeed required (see below) – for medical professionals literally to treat people as though they were merely bodies in these cases, what sort of "firewall" do advocates of such permission suggest to prevent the spread of such treatment to other areas of social life, together with the attitudes and beliefs it both requires and encourages? They offer no such proposals.

Nor is it just the obvious features of a slippery slope – such as enforced sterilization and castration, the medical experiments "for the greater good" familiar from the annals of Nazism – that they fail to address. They ignore wider, everyday and entirely obvious consequences. The impact on the wider 'laws of war', which 'defer to medical ethics', [94] would also be disastrous. And just imagine being treated by an anaesthetist or a surgeon who only yesterday was "assisting" in torture.

A Torturous Society

The issue of spread is critical, not least since, if the proposals we have been examining were sound, their conclusions would in fact be far stronger than any of their proponents acknowledge. It is not just that interrogational torture in ticking bomb scenarios would become morally permissible, or come to be seen as such, as the result of its legalization; it would become, or come to be seen as, a moral duty. Such a duty, moreover, would extend to doctors, nurses, lawyers, judges and many other "support staff". To see why, let us go back to the train driver. Their choice, remember, is between mowing down a busload of children and mowing down a drunk. On a utilitarian view, however, the driver is not morally *permitted*, but morally *required*, to mow down the drunk: for that action is *right* which leads to the greatest happiness of the greatest number, or the consequences of which are least bad. If the train driver chose not to mow down the drunk, which as the example is set up means that she would mow down the children, then her choice would be morally wrong. It is not a matter merely of being *permitted*, in the circumstances, to mow down the drunk; it is what the train driver *must* do. In the same way, it is not simply that interrogators, having obtained a warrant, are permitted to use torture; they are *required* to use torture, just because it is the only way, according to the terms of the ticking bomb scenario, of – perhaps – avoiding the worst consequences. Utilitarianism has no logical space for mere moral permissibility (except, of course, in the case of equally beneficial consequences): doing what has the best consequences is what is morally required, simply because on a utilitarian account 'has the best consequences' means 'morally right'. Thus, if the grounds on which interrogational torture is permitted are exigency, the necessity to obtain the required information, then it is in fact *required*, and not merely permitted. It becomes "our" – or our delegated surrogates' – *duty* to torture. Advocates of interrogational torture and/or its legalization are not alone in failing to notice this; many of their opponents also fail to notice it. [95] But it is a crucial point. If the *only* way of avoiding consequences that, on moral grounds, *must* be avoided is to torture, then such torture is not merely permitted, it is required. The end is, as the example stands, something we have to try to attain; torture is, again as the example stands, the only means available; therefore we must adopt it. (Again, Dershowitz's critics might be forgiven for taking him to be advocating interrogational torture, since he appears not to see this implication of his "train driver" approach to the issue.)

That takes us back to the issue of agency. We have already seen that no one bothers explicitly to address the question of who is to carry out the "required" torture. But this now turns out to be an even more urgent question than when I raised it earlier. For if torturing suspects under certain conditions is a duty, then the question arises of whose duty it is. And since neither lawyers nor philosophers – nor many members of the public – are trained torturers, we have to ask on what grounds we are justified in urging a moral *duty* upon others which we ourselves are not prepared either to improvise or to undergo the required "moral training" adequately to fulfil – provided, of course, that we do not lack the necessary abilities through no fault of our own. Now, as we have seen, Posner, among others, argues that 'No one who doubts' that interrogational torture is in certain circumstances justified 'should be in a position of public responsibility'; [96] it is simply hypocritical, they think, to shy away from the necessities of reality. But that argument can now be turned back against the advocates of torture. Is it not hypocritical – or worse – to expect public officials to torture people if you are not prepared to do it yourself? Of course, we all of us expect others to do things we ourselves would shy away from: doctors, nurses, dentists, mortuary attendants and a host of others. But it is one thing to shy away from doing what you expect other people to do for you, or on your behalf, and quite another not to be prepared in principle to undergo the requisite training for what you think is a morally *required* job, rather than one which is morally merely permissible. If you really think that capital punishment is morally necessary, that it is society's moral duty to impose the death penalty for certain crimes, then if you would not under any circumstances be prepared to learn to act as executioner – assuming you had the capacity to do so – you are being hypocritical. If you think that assisted suicide is a moral right, so that someone or other has a concomitant moral duty so to assist in certain circumstances, then, provided you are able, you have to be willing to do so yourself.

If it is the case that interrogational torture in ticking bomb circumstances is morally justifiable, then it is no less the case that torture is in those circumstances morally required. It becomes a moral duty to torture. It is in that light that I offer the words of a professional torturer:

> Finally, I went forward to look at his face and closely examined his condition. I realized that he had lost his mental balance. We removed him from the torture bench and instead hung him from special handcuffs installed on the wall. [97]

How dare anyone seek even by implication to impose such a duty on others, whether they are academics or those 'audiences' asked 'for a show of hands' [98], to indicate support for "the lesser of two evils"?

Chapter Four

Torture, Death and Philosophy

I have argued that the ticking bomb scenario is a fantasy, and thus cannot serve as any sort of basis for public policy; and that legalizing interrogational torture, far from limiting its use, would lead to its spread, as well as being counterproductive in other ways. But still, even if you agree with my assessment of the likely consequences of legalizing interrogational torture in respect of normalizing the practice of torture, you may think that, although it ought not to be legalized, it should nevertheless sometimes be retrospectively condoned. That is to say, you may not agree that the ticking bomb scenario is as extreme a fantasy as I painted it to be in chapter two, and that thinkers like Nussbaum, Posner and Walzer are therefore right about interrogational torture's being justifiable in certain extreme cases, even though it should remain illegal. So I want now to think about what torture is, and why – even on a utilitarian view – it is wrong, always and everywhere.

I shall argue that torture *breaks* people; and that "purely" interrogational torture, something that 'leaves no lasting damage', is thus yet another fantasy. To allow torture at all, therefore – whether or not legally normalized – would be grotesque. In light of that, I shall go on to suggest, intellectuals need to exercise particular responsibility about how they use their imaginations when they address these matters. Finally, I shall say something about the bottom line in all this: where torture really does at least *appear* to be the only possible way of preventing catastrophe then it is already too late. Trying in those circumstances to prevent catastrophe would require that we accept a greater and deeper disaster.

Torture

In the opening chapter, I offered Christopher Tindale's view of torture as

> any act by which severe pain or suffering, whether physical or mental, is intentionally inflicted on a person for such purposes as obtaining from that person or a third person information or confession, punishing that person for an act committed or suspected to have been committed, or intimidating or dehumanizing that person or other persons. [1]

On a more everyday level, however (not interrogation, but the sort of sadism that children sometimes indulge in) torture is simply, as Barrie Paskins puts it, 'the systematic and deliberate infliction of acute pain in any form by one person on another'. [2] This adds something important to Tindale's more formal characterization: the notion that torture is something carried out *systematically*. It is something purposeful, something formal; it has aims and a structure; it is not gratuitous. It is not *just any* cruelty, not *just any* infliction of 'severe pain or suffering'.

So what sort of act is torture? What sort of intention is an intention systematically to inflict 'severe pain or suffering' on a person? I am not asking *what* the torturer intends to achieve by torture but rather *how* such intentions might be realized. Let me start with Robert Cover's comment that torture is the 'deliberate infliction of pain in order to destroy the victim's normative world and capacity to create shared realities'. [3] Pain itself is not enough: it has to be of a sort and of an intensity to achieve something very specific. The intention is to destroy the victim's normative relation to the torturer, and thus to themselves as a person: to make the victim into something that is no longer a person. Alone with their torturers, treated by them not as a person but as an object, human beings cease to be persons. That is what people mean when they talk of torture "breaking" the tortured:

> The subject of judicial or interrogational torture is "broken" when, and only when, he has become so distraught, so unable to bear any more suffering, that he can no longer resist any request the torturer might make. The tortured then "pours out his guts". [4]

The tortured person's capacity to act is broken. And since it is our capacity to act which makes us persons, rather than just instances of a particular biological species – however heavily circumscribed that capacity might be under certain circumstances – the tortured subject is no longer a person. [5] Jean Améry, speaking as a person who in one sense survived torture, makes the point better than I ever could:

> Only in torture does the transformation of the person into flesh become complete. Frail in the face of violence, yelling out in pain, awaiting no help, capable of no resistance, the tortured person is only a body, and nothing else besides that. [6]

I want to think more about what Améry says. Let me start with a very obvious question. Why is it that none of the advocates of interrogational torture or of its legalization that I have come across make any reference at all to Améry's testimony? His essay, 'Torture', is, after all, the single best-known work of its sort. You might think that anyone discussing torture would need to say something about what it actually is. In fairness, Dershowitz at least attempts to say *something* about the torture he has in mind – needles under the fingernails. Like direct advocates of interrogational torture, however, he is either unable or unwilling to face up to what torture actually is in his insouciant description of what he has in mind. I wonder why? Might it be that it makes a nonsense of any notion of torture as something 'designed to cause excruciating pain without leaving any lasting damage'? [7] Listen again to Améry.

He tells us that 'What was inflicted on me in the unspeakable vault in Breendonk was by far not the worst form of torture'. [8] I shall return to the question of "degrees" of torture presently. While not 'the worst', this is what the Nazis did to Améry:

> In the bunker there hung from the vaulted ceiling a chain that above ran into a roll. At its bottom end it bore a heavy, broadly curved iron hook. I was led to the instrument. The hook gripped into the shackle that held my hands together behind my back. Then I was raised with the chain until I hung about a meter over the floor. In such a position, or rather, when hanging this way, with your hands behind your back, for a short time you can hold at a half-oblique through muscular force. . . . But this cannot last long, even with people who have a strong physical constitution. As for me, I had to give up rather quickly. And

now there was a crackling and splintering in my shoulders that my body has not forgotten until this hour. The balls sprang from their sockets. My own body weight caused luxation; I fell into a void and now hung by my dislocated arms, which had been torn high from behind and were now twisted over my head. Torture, from Latin *torquere*, to twist. [9]

Améry goes on to speak about what '*my body has not forgotten until this hour*'. You might ask why. Améry tells us: the pain was such as to be indescribable. 'The pain was what it was. Beyond that there is nothing to say. Qualities of feeling are as incomparable as they are indescribable. They mark the limit of the capacity of language to communicate.' [10] No wonder that it cannot be forgotten: 'It was over for a while. It still is not over. Twenty-two years later I am still dangling over the ground by dislocated arms, panting, and accusing myself.' [11] It is not only because of the pain that the torture stays with him, Améry says: for even 'The first blow brings home to the prisoner that he is helpless, and thus it already contains in the bud everything that is to come'. [12] It is the experience of utter helplessness that is central; and it is the torturer's job to make their victim utterly helpless. Why? Because 'The expectation of help, the certainty of help, is indeed one of the fundamental experiences of human beings'. [13] Take that expectation away from someone, and they are broken; something integral to their being a person is missing. That, Améry tells us, is why 'with the first blow from a policeman's fist, against which there can be no defense and which no helping hand will ward off, a part of our life ends and it can never again be revived'. [14] That, Améry tells anyone willing to listen, is why 'Whoever has succumbed to torture can no longer feel at home in the world. The shame of destruction cannot be erased. Trust in the world, which already collapsed in part at the first blow, but in the end, under torture, fully, will not be regained.' [15] Thirty-three years after being released from the site of the last of his tortures, on 17 October 1978, Jean Améry committed suicide.

Améry had not been at home in the world since Breendonk. For in breaking a person's body, the torturer breaks the person. Thinking about torture is in fact one way of showing how body and person are co-implied. [16] I said earlier that Améry had survived torture 'in one sense'. What I meant is that the "he" who had survived was not the same person as before; under torture, his body was no longer his own, and that experience remained. In remaining, it made him into a different person. In the course of his treatment by another as not a person, his relation to his own self, as well as to others, had been shattered; his torture was now part of the person he was, and he could not "go back to who he had been". Notice in particular the first point here, about how Améry was treated 'as not a person'. In order to achieve that, his torturers had to *start*, at least, by treating him in one sense as a person. Only by initially *recognizing* him as a person – as a being whose body is integral to their identity – could they go on to break him by breaking his body. It is the *whole* of the process of torture in which treating him as not a person consisted; and to describe it as such is already to make a normative claim that no person *ought* to be treated like that. Why not? Because, and this claim is a factual one, it breaks them, it destroys the person they are. Améry's torturers, that is to say, turned his personhood against him, and in doing so made him into someone else. That is how he survived, as someone else; others do not. It is also why he eventually killed himself.

Torture, Death and Interrogation

In light of that, how should we understand the conception of torture that proponents of interrogational torture and/or its legalization appear to have? I shall first look at the little they actually say, and then consider a defence they might offer, namely that *interrogational* torture is quite different from other sorts of torture.

Torture and death

Dershowitz insists that 'Pain is a lesser and more remediable harm than death': [17] others assume it. Explicit though it is, his reliance on a comparison with the death penalty to bolster his argument remains entirely unexamined. He simply invites his readers to consider 'What moral principle could justify the death penalty for past individual murders and at the same time condemn nonlethal torture to prevent future mass murders?' [18] One obvious response is to remind him that abolishing the death penalty is far from unrealistic, and has actually been achieved across a considerable portion of the world. Whatever your views on that, however, you might be inclined to agree that death is surely worse than torture; and that killing a person is therefore worse than torturing them. After all, provided that a particular torture is indeed non-lethal (Dershowitz's 'sterilized needle', [19] for example), the person tortured is at least still alive. Ghastly beyond ordinary imagination though the experience was, they are not dead. That is certainly Seumas Miller's argument:

> It does not follow that torture is less preferable than being killed because the duration of the torture might be brief, one's will might not ultimately be broken, and one might go on to live a long and happy life; by contrast, being killed – theological considerations aside – is always 'followed by' no life whatsoever. [20]

But Miller, though at least he attempts the beginnings of an argument, assumes too much.

I shall not question his putting the point in terms of preference, since my argument against torture is not about moral *theory*. [21] But his view that torture which was relatively short and which did not ultimately break one's will might well be preferable to death is deeply problematic in other ways. For some people death is preferable to torture, not just while being tortured, but afterwards too, 'theological considerations' or not; and despite its relative mildness. Just listen to the testimony of contemporary survivors of torture – and of its close relation, rape – in Rwanda, Kenya, the Congo, the Balkans and all too many other places. More importantly, the whole point of the interrogational torture at issue here is that it is supposed to be extremely effective, since the ticking bomb situation is one of extreme urgency. Miller thus ignores the obvious question: what if it turns out that one's will *is* broken, and that one's life *is* irretrievably shattered? As Améry reminds us, in that case *who* one is has changed; and how one relates to that self is now problematic, where once it was not. There are two problems here. First, on a fairly simple level, Miller forgets to tell us whether his assessment of what is preferable relates to the situation before torture begins or after it is over. If it is a matter of a person's preference before the torture starts, then they might well prefer – or judge – death to be better than *the risk* of one's will being broken and/or of one's life being irretrievably shattered. If the preference Miller has in mind is one expressed once the torture is over, then it is quite possible that neither preference nor judgement are any longer relevant. For these are components of a normal human life, not of an entirely shattered one. The inability in any everyday sense to prefer one thing to another, and/or to make everyday judgements, is precisely part of what it is for one's life to have been utterly shattered. That is why some people might consider the risk of such a "life" not worth taking. As Michael Davis reminds us, it is not for nothing that for traditional Christians 'Hell, the ultimate punishment, is eternal life at the price of eternal torment'. [22] Again, the thought goes beyond any religious outlook, as the evidence of survivors of torture attests. Second, at a deeper level, his thinking assumes a notion of a person as something that can survive the loss of bodily integrity – of my body as "mine", however exactly that is conceptualized – without radical rupture: 'one might go on to live a long and happy life'. Again, Améry shows that this notion of what a person is – something essentially fixed and independent of the body – is unsustainable.

That is why the assumption that death is always, and for everyone, the worst possible fate, is unwarranted. The conception of what a person is that underlies it is naïve. It is, however, widely shared. [23] It certainly underlies Dershowitz's extraordinary understanding of torture as something that might consist in 'judicially monitored physical measures designed to cause excruciating pain *without leaving any lasting damage*'. [24] Lasting damage is not a matter solely of physical scars, or even of what are generally understood as psychological ones. The pain does not simply disappear, leaving intact the essentially unchanged person. We know that from people's experience of accidents and illness. Excruciating pain inflicted by another as a means of imposing their will on you goes even deeper, however. It is something that changes you entirely at another's behest. No wonder it can destroy the person you thereby become. Deliberately and systematically inflicted by others, such pain changes in particular how you respond to others. We know that from Améry, from Elie Wiesel, [25] from Istvan Kertész [26] and from countless victims of what we might term, euphemistically, the involuntary use of their bodies by others.

Interrogational torture and "torture lite"

But it might be replied that both Améry's testimony, and the other reports to which I have referred, deeply disturbing though they are, nonetheless miss the point. Torture as actually practised in its various forms is doubtless often like that; but interrogational torture, strictly limited and designed solely to elicit specific and urgently required information, is quite different. What else could explain Posner's repellent accusation against Ariel Dorfman's moving foreword to Levinson's collection on torture – where he hopes that 'humanity will have the courage to say no, no to torture, no to torture under any circumstances whatsoever' [27] – that it 'is not only overwrought in tone but irresponsible in content'? [28] What I am advocating, he must be thinking, is interrogational torture only – and then only in very specific, tightly circumscribed circumstances. These testimonies, and others like them, do not concern the nature and effects of highly focused and reluctantly applied interrogational torture. They are responses to intimidatory, vengeful and/or sadistic torture; to prolonged torture carried out specifically with the aim of breaking the prisoner entirely. Interrogational torture in the ticking bomb context is by design short, sharp and strictly limited. It aims only to break the prisoner to the extent required to get the information needed. Furthermore, they might add, these testimonies – like Dorfman's – concern the torture of innocent people, or at least people innocent of planting bombs in public places, even if they are members of a resistance or oppositional movement. Well, we have already looked at the obvious "slippery slope" issues about how "realistic" it is to suppose that such "intelligent torture" – modelled, it would seem, on "smart" bombs and missiles – would not *lead to* more and different torture. That is not the point here, however. Rather, the question is whether what has been hideously termed "torture lite" is a realistic possibility.

Awful though it is, we have to consider such a response and the distinction it relies on. First, both the advocates of interrogational torture and those of its legalization are in fairness owed that consideration. Second, it is important to see that their case cannot be salvaged in this way.

Seamus Miller makes the idea admirably explicit:

> The difference between minimalist and maximalist torture is that in the former case the victim's will is broken only temporarily and in a contained manner, and their consequent humiliation is limited, i.e., they survive the trauma and are able to get on with their lives. However, in the maximalist case the victim's autonomy and self-identity are damaged irretrievably. Accordingly, the victim – even if alive and physically well – has not survived intact qua autonomous self. [29]

Whether or not it reflects his own view, we can understand Miller's distinction as one that recognizes what I have been saying about the person and our relation to our bodies, but denies that all torture has the sort of impact I have described. 'Minimalist' torture leaves the person intact; those subjected to it 'survive the trauma' much as we might survive an operation; their will, and body, are both, so to speak, returned to them and they can "start again" as the person they were.

The problem with that distinction, however, is that it simply assumes that the difference between a broken and an unbroken will – a shattered person and one who can be repaired – is a matter of kind rather than of degree. It is as if one could point to *that* torture – a needle under the fingernails, perhaps, to return to Dershowitz – and say that it is 'minimalist'; and to some other torture – genital and other mutilation, perhaps – and say that that is 'maximalist'. But I have to ask: how many fingernails; for how long? The idea that these are different *sorts* of torture, rather than different *degrees* of it, is unsubstantiated, a judgement that Améry's testimony confirms. On his own account, his torture was 'not the worst'; and yet it broke him. Or would anyone deny that Améry was in fact broken, because he went on to produce wonderful writing and killed himself "only" thirty-three years later?

Still, even if I am wrong about that, how might the distinction work in practice? If 'minimalist' torture were not enough to get the information, how likely is it that the torture would stop before it became 'maximalist'? Clearly, Dershowitz himself is committed to drawing the line at the former (torture must leave 'no lasting damage'). Presumably, therefore, torture which would – or might? – result in 'lasting damage' is ruled out. So if 'minimalist' torture were insufficient, the interrogators and torturers would just have to leave the bomb to explode – as the "suspect" would know all along. Furthermore, the judicial torture warrant, permitting only 'minimalist' torture, would of course be sufficient to halt the professional torturers in their tracks: the law must be obeyed, after all. The whole idea is ridiculous.

The other possibility would be for advocates of interrogational torture and/or its legalization openly to argue that 'maximalist' torture is justifiable in the ticking bomb scenario – perhaps because the suspect's guilt is, allegedly, clear. That would certainly be a more "realistic" position, not least since the scenario depends on established guilt. Or at least, it would be more realistic to the extent that 'maximal' torture is compatible with the "suspect's" remaining enough of a person to be interrogated at all: you cannot interrogate a being unable to communicate with you. While most advocates of torture are not explicit about this, Dershowitz himself rules out 'maximal' torture. He is clear that, even if his proposal were accepted, bombs would still explode, since the restrictions he himself imposes on projected torture warrants mean that only a small proportion of ticking bombs would be found in time. As we have seen, to avoid that – to make his "modest proposal" genuinely "realistic" – would require the legalization of torture beyond what he thinks would leave no lasting damage; of the torture of others beside the "suspect" alone, and of others known to be innocent; and of torture intended to forestall ticking bombs by gleaning information in advance. What sort of society would it be that sanctioned that, whether openly and legally, or "after the event" and despite its illegality?

Why No Decent Society Can Torture

Let me summarize my argument in this chapter so far. However artfully and artificially the notion of purely interrogational torture is presented, as something directed solely at the "guilty" suspect and – at least so far as some are concerned – leaving no lasting damage, that cannot mask what torture is. It is 'a crime of specific intent: It involves the use of pain deliberately and specifically to *break the will* of the subject.' [30] The torturous society we would thus create would be so grotesque, in so many related ways, as to outweigh the benefit of *sometimes possibly* avoiding the catastrophe of the ticking bomb. How do we know that? Well, imagine what such a society would look like. Not that we have to rely solely on imagination: we are busily creating such societies already, and the proposal to legalize interrogational torture is so appalling because – for all that it is presented as a radical challenge – it in fact serves to justify what we are doing.

Why is such a society grotesque? David Luban's aptly Orwellian thought focuses attention on what it is we ask people to do if we ask them to torture people on our behalf: now torture 'to gather intelligence and save lives seems almost heroic. For the first time, we can think of kindly torturers.' [31] And with that thought, we would already have lost too much. For as Naomi Klein reminds us, the 'true purpose' of torture is 'to terrorize – not only the people in Guantanamo's cages and Syria's isolation cells but also, and more importantly, the broader community that hears about these abuses. Torture is a machine designed to break the will to resist – the individual prisoner's will and the collective will.' [32] If people were cost-benefit machines concerned only to maximize whatever they took benefit to be, they could perhaps live and take an active part in a society which sanctioned that. [33] That is not what we are, however. As we have seen in the assumptions they make about torture being just obviously preferable to death, the consequentialism of the advocates of torture and/or its legalization is a very particular form of such a conception of morality. So even apart from all the detailed shortcomings of their arguments, their conclusions do not *automatically* follow, even on a consequentialist view of right and wrong. You can be a consequentialist and *still* think that there is some 'form of survival which is not worth the effort'; [34] that a society in which breaking people by torture were institutionalized, normalized and recognized as a valuable service is one not worth having. Go back to the quotation with which I began the previous chapter.

Torture, the "War on Terror" and Intellectual Irresponsibility

So how on earth have avowedly civilized people got to the point where we are seriously debating the normalization of torture? Other writers, such as Luban, [35] have traced some of the political story of the role of the "ticking bomb" and its allegedly justifying interrogational torture in the so-called war on terror. Jeremy Waldron [36] has performed a major service in his analysis of the legal story. And Richard Jackson [37] in particular has alerted us to how the deliberate distortion of language manipulates people into contemplating what is beyond the pale. I want to add just a brief word about the role of philosophers. It is a statement of the obvious, although it seems to have been anything but obvious to those concerned. Thought-experiments are one thing; the real world is another. And while thought-experiments on their own can help us *think about the limits of philosophical theories*, such as utilitarianism, they *tell us nothing about the world*. Recall Elshtain's "bomb in a school" example (chapter two). It is crucial, therefore, that those who use them take great care lest they permit others to pretend otherwise. Two things are especially important. First, what "you" or "I" think we would do is one thing, and especially where we were directly involved ("What if your child was kidnapped?"); what ought to be done, and by whom, is another. Second, where thought-experiments *seem* at least to touch on the real world, philosophers had better take great care to know what they are talking about – as we have seen regarding the ticking bomb scenario and now regarding torture. Any justificatory power they have comes from the real world, not from the thought-experiment alone. It is the way the world is that makes something right or wrong.

Strangely perhaps, it is its insouciance about the real world which characterizes the "new realism" both of the advocates of interrogational torture and of its legalization. Nonetheless, the story of their proposal is a story of the irresponsibility no less of philosophers who play with the "ticking bomb" in careless thought-experiments than of the lawyers who take advantage of them. Intellectuals, I think, do have a particular responsibility to engage in public life. [38] But they have also a particular responsibility not to do so carelessly, and to remember that, however they conceptualize it, reality is not something that should be made to serve the purposes of fantasy – whether in the hands of philosophers or, far more dangerously, of politicians.

But What if Torture Really is the Only Possible Way to Avoid Catastrophe?

The ticking bomb scenario, presented in a context of terrorism, is a fantasy. But that is not to say that there can be no genuine cases where torturing one person seems the only possible way left of saving the life of one or more others and where it really is known that they have the requisite information. Doris Schroeder's recent analysis of the Gäfgen case in Germany in 2002 offers one example. Having collected evidence from his flat and watched him collect the ransom, the police knew that Magnus Gäfgen had kidnapped Jakob von Metzler, the 11-year-old son of a banker. He refused to say where the boy was. Knowing that he might be slowly dying, the police president 'ordered his men to threaten Gäfgen with violence to force a statement'. [39] That was enough to elicit what he knew. Unhappily, though, the boy was already dead. As

Schroeder outlines, the case provoked an impassioned debate about torture in Germany. There was no consensus. [40] Here is another case, this time fictional. A person who is clearly mentally ill (and however we understand that) walks into a police station and says they have planted a bomb in a public place, timed to explode in three hours. To make sure they are taken seriously, they say they have also planted a smaller bomb in a particular shopping arcade, timed to explode in five minutes. It does so. They refuse to say where the second bomb is. In both these cases, just those conditions apply which did not in those apparently involving dedicated terrorists. So what is to be done? Remember that the question is not, "What would you do (if you were the boy's mother; if you happened to find yourself at the police interrogation)?" The question is about public policy and what is right and wrong, not about individuals' likely emotional reactions.

Nothing is to be done. It is too late. If *legal* torture were sanctioned, then we would have to accept all the consequences we have already considered. What is necessary to institutionalize interrogational torture, however, is unacceptable. If *illegal* torture were sanctioned – as of course in the real world it is – then, while the legal and many of the other consequences we have considered would not come into play, those concerning the acceptance and the spread of torture would. That is exactly what the experience of Israel shows and what Dershowitz himself rightly argues against the hypocrisy of "justification after the event" and despite the law. Either way, torture cannot be justified. As Michael Ignatieff recently put it, after earlier prevarication,

> democracies limit the powers that governments can justly exercise over the human beings under their power, and these limits include an absolute ban on subjecting individuals to forms of pain that strip them of their dignity, identity, and even sanity.
> We cannot torture, in other words, because of who we are. [41]

Who we are places limits on the sort of society in which we can live. To the extent that utilitarians acknowledge this at all, they are mistaken about who we are, as I have argued. So one of those limits is that not every catastrophe that could perhaps be avoided should be avoided. In fact, of course, most of us accept this principle already, whether implicitly as citizens of our societies, or more explicitly as individuals. We could avoid all road accidents; but we do not. We could avoid the death by starvation of many children around the world; but we do not. We could prevent the killing and maiming of untold numbers of innocent civilians round the world; but we do not. Rightly or wrongly, that is how we judge the benefits of inaction. In the case of torture, though, inaction is right. The very occasional catastrophe (and remember that legalizing interrogational torture might, just possibly, prevent only a tiny fraction even of real terrorist actions) is a price we have to pay to avoid creating a torturous society. We need to do what we can to eliminate the conditions which give rise to bombs, ticking or not. If we fail, then it is too late. And the two very different sorts of case I have just alluded to need to be understood along the lines of natural disasters, akin more to earthquakes than to the actions of determined terrorists. They offer no basis for public policy regarding terrorist bombs. However terrible for everyone concerned, they really are unavoidable on pain of the greater catastrophe of a torturous society.

Two Final Points

Let me finish with two brief points. The first is a reminder about the substantive issue of torture. If I am right that interrogational torture is ruled out absolutely, then as I suggested at the outset, *all* torture is ruled out. The second concerns the utilitarian framework I have adopted in order to take on proponents of interrogational torture on their own terms. My excuse for doing that, and I hope a justification, is that I had to get my hands intellectually dirty if I was to offer arguments that stood a chance of being listened to. While I think that an analysis of their arguments illustrates as comprehensively as anything could the bankruptcy of a view of morality which looks solely to the consequences of what we do, what really matters is this. In the end, the conclusion that all torture is wrong, always and everywhere, follows *even on that view*. You do not have to be a moral absolutist to argue for an absolute rejection of torture, or of its legalization. Still, if I have indirectly persuaded anyone that torture is wrong, full stop, just because *it is torture*, then so much the better.

Notes

Preface

1 Gearty, Conor (2005) Legitimizing torture – with a little help from our friends, *Index on Censorship 1/05: Torture – a user's manual,* available at www.indexonline.org/en/news/articles/2005/1/international-legitimising-torture-with-a-li.shtml.

Chapter 1 Introduction

1 Bybee, Jay S. (2002) Memorandum for Alberto R. Gonzales, Counsel to the President, re: Standards of Conduct for Interrogation under 18 U.S.C. (1 August): in Danner, Mark (2004b) *Torture and Truth: America, Abu Ghraib, and the War on Terror,* New York Review of Books, New York, 115–166. Officially, the memorandum was repudiated: 'in fact, large sections were incorporated more or less verbatim' into a Working Group Report 'set up in the Pentagon in January 2003 to reconsider interrogation methods' – Waldron, Jeremy (2005) Torture and positive law: jurisprudence for the White House, *Columbia Law Review,* 105, 1681–1750, p. 1704. The currently definitive set of publicly available official US government and military papers concerning the role of torture in the "war on terror" is Greenberg, Karen and Dratel, Joshua (eds.) (2005) *The Torture Papers,* Cambridge University Press, Cambridge. A new edition is in preparation at the time of writing.

2 Shue, Henry (1978) Torture, *Philosophy and Public Affairs,* 7, 124–143, p. 124. Reprinted in Levinson, S. (ed.) (2004), 47–60. William Twining also ponders the risks of even debating torture: Twining, W. (1978) Torture and philosophy, *Proceedings of the Aristotelian Society,* 52 (Supplement), 143–168.

3 Žižek, Slavoj (2002) *Welcome to the Desert of the Real,* Verso, London, 103: quoted by Levinson, Sanford (2004) Contemplating torture: an introduction: in Levinson, S. (ed.) (2004) *Torture: A Collection,* Oxford University Press, Oxford, 23–43, p. 30.

4   Harbury, Jennifer (2005) *Truth, Torture, and the American Way: The History and Consequences of US Involvement in Torture*, Beacon Press, Boston. My thanks to Will Podmore for alerting me to this excoriating indictment.

5   See Grey, Stephen and Cobain, Ian (2006) From logistics to turning a blind eye: Europe's role in terror abduction, the *Guardian*, 7 June: available at www.guardian.co.uk. For a useful review of how the United States government came to try to "redefine" torture and a brief argument that its legalization would undermine the very democracy it purports to buttress, see Lukes, Steven (2006) Liberal democratic torture, *British Journal of Political Science*, 36, 1–16.

6   Scheppele, Kim Lane (2005) Hypothetical torture in the "war on terrorism", *Journal of National Security Law and Policy*, 1, 285–340, p. 286. For a succinct summary of how the scene has been set by lawyers and philosophers, see Bufacchi, Vittorio and Arrigo, Jean Maria (2006) Tortured reasoning, *Journal of Applied Philosophy* 23, 355–373, pp. 357–359. Their excellent paper, which I saw only shortly before my own manuscript was due at the publisher's, is a concise statement of a position similar to the one I develop here.

7   Bagaric, Mirko and Clarke, Julie (2005) Not enough official torture in the world? The circumstances in which torture is morally justifiable, *University of San Francisco Law Review* 39, 581–616. They are quite explicit: 'We argue that torture is indeed morally defensible, not just pragmatically desirable' – 582–583. The quotations are from the report of its publication in the *Times Higher Education Supplement* (2005), Make torture legal, say law academics, 27 May, 14.

8   Jackson, Richard (2005b) *Writing the War on Terrorism: Language, Politics and Counter-terrorism*, Manchester University Press, Manchester.

9   In (controversial) philosophical terms, types are not real things.

10 Tindale, Christopher (1996) The logic of torture, *Social Theory and Practice*, 22, 349–374, p. 351. See Waldron, J. (2005), 1688ff., for an extremely fine treatment of the issue of definition.

11 Amnesty International (2004) *United States of America: Human Dignity Denied – torture and accountability in the "war on terror"*: AI Index AMR 51/145/2004, 17.

12 Bybee, Jay S. (2002), 120.

13 Roth, Kenneth (2005) Justifying Torture, in Roth, K. and Worden, M. (eds.) (2005), 184–202, p. 194, quoting Jehl, Douglas (2005) Questions are left by CIA chief on the use of torture, *New York Times*, 18 March, Section A, 1, col. 5.

14 Gonzales, Alberto (2004) Press briefing by White House Counsel Judge Alberto Gonzales, DOD [Department of Defense] General Counsel William Haynes, DOD Deputy general Counsel Danile Dell'Orto and Army Deputy Chief of Staff for Intelligence General Keith Alexander, 22 June: available at www.whitehouse.gov/news/releases/2004/06/20040622–14.html, quoted in *Amnesty International Report* (2004), 15. As it points out, this was not the only aspect of the US administration's cynicism on this. It also 'sanctioned interrogation techniques that, even if each of them did not amount to torture in themselves, have done so in combination . . .' – 17.

15 Available at: www.un.org/documents/ga/res/39/a39r046.htm.

16   For an account of how various legal definitions are subject to quite rapid change about the "threshold" of torture, see Evans, Malcolm (2002) Getting to grips with torture, *International and Comparative Law Quarterly*, 51, 365–383, pp. 370–375: ironically, however, he then goes on to say that 'it is with relief that one turns to the UNCAT, Article 1, which provides a definition' – 375. See also Waldron, J. (2005), 1688–1703, and especially 1687: 'Give us a definition so we have something to work around, something to *game*, a determinate envelope to push.' Why do so many lawyers apparently not see this? Seth Kreimer is a notable exception: see Kreimer, Seth (2003) Too close to the rack and screw, *University of Pennsylvania Journal of Constitutional Law*, 6, 278–325.

17   The example is Waldron's: Waldron, J. (2005), 1700. As he goes on to say, the search for a (precise) definition is reasonable in cases where there is a genuine interest in thresholds on some *legitimate* continuum or other (speed limits, tax-exempt donations). But the continuum on which torture is to be found is that of cruel and inhuman treatment, the legitimacy of which is exactly what is at issue. Imagine, Waldron suggests, a 'husband who says "I have an interest in pushing my wife round a bit and I need to know exactly how far I can go before it counts as domestic violence"' – 1701.

18   Tindale, C. (1996), 355. See 354–355 for why he (rightly, in my view) wants slightly to modify the UN formulation.

19   Dershowitz, Alan (2002c) *Why Terrorism Works*, Yale University Press, New Haven and London. See also his (2002b) *Shouting Fire: Civil Liberties in a Turbulent Age,* Little Brown, New York, 470–477.

20   Dershowitz, Alan (2004c) When torture is the least evil of terrible options, *Times Higher Education Supplement*, 11 June, 20–21.

21   Bentham, Jeremy, Of torture, Bentham MSS Box 46, 63–70; 56–62: both reproduced in Twining, W. L. and Twining, P. E. (1973) Bentham on torture, *Northern Ireland Legal Quarterly*, 24, 307–356.

22   Dershowitz, A. (2004c), 20.

23   Dershowitz, A. (2002c), 163.

24   For details, see Biletzki, Anat (2001) The judicial rhetoric of morality: Israel's High Court of Justice on the legality of torture, unpublished paper, 12: available at www.sss.ias.edu/publications/papers/papernine/pdf. The Israeli Supreme Court's 1999 'Judgement on the interrogation methods applied by the GSS' clearly and unambiguously admits this. It states, for example, that 'the GSS also investigates those suspected of hostile terrorist activities. The purpose of these interrogations is, *among others*, to gather information regarding terrorists and their organizing methods for the purpose of thwarting and preventing them from carrying out these terrorist attacks.' – 3, my emphasis. The judgement is available at www.derechos.org/human-rights/mena/doc/torture.html. What appear to Biletzki and others to be its ambiguities regarding 'Physical Means and the "Necessity" Defence' (17ff.), for all that it was popularly taken to have stopped torture *tout court*, are explored in detail in Biletzki (2001), which is, among other things, an excellent critique of much of Dershowitz's case.

25   Dershowitz, A. (2002c), 140.

26 Dershowitz, Alan (1989) Is it necessary to apply "physical pressure" to terrorists – and to lie about it?, *Israel Law Review* 23, 192–200.

27 Biletzki, A. (2001), 13.

28 Dershowitz, Alan (2001) Is there a torturous road to justice?, 8 November; available at www.groups-beta.google.com/group/alt.impeach.bush/msg/814527884aa6c904.

29 Dershowitz, Alan (2006b) Should we fight terror with torture?, *Independent* 3 July (unpaginated): available at www.independent.co.uk. The book in which he develops his argument is Dershowitz, Alan (2006a) *Preemption: A Knife That Cuts Both Ways*, Norton, New York.

30 Dershowitz (2002c), 150. A more recent real poll (*USA Today/CNN/Gallup Poll Results*, 12 January 2005) offers more hope, reporting that '59 per cent of respondents said they would *not* approve the US government's torturing of *known terrorists*, even if those known terrorists "know details about future terrorist attacks in the US" and the government thinks such torture is "necessary to combat terrorism"': cited by Scheppele, K. (2005), 292, n. 17, and available at www.usatoday.com//news/polls/tables/live/2005–01–10–poll.htm.

31 Biletzki, A. (2001), 10.

32 See, to take just two examples, Heffer, Simon (2005) Our lunatic laws just help Al Qaeda, *Daily Mail*, 23 July and editorial comment (2005) Deadly times, deadly action, the *Sun*, 23 July. For an excellent analysis of the ticking bomb scenario as an expression of liberal ideology and of the political implications of that being the case, see Luban, David (2005) Liberalism, torture, and the ticking bomb, *Virginia Law Review*, 91, 1425–1461. My thanks to an anonymous reviewer for alerting me to Luban's brilliant article.

33 Nussbaum, Martha, quoted by Press, Eyal (2003) Tortured logic: thumbscrewing international law, *Amnesty Magazine*, summer, 2: available at www.amnestyusa.org/magazine/tortured/html.

34 Posner, Richard (2004) Torture, terrorism, and interrogation, in Levinson, S. (ed.) (2004), 291–298, p. 295.

35 Parry, John (2004) Escalation and necessity: defining torture at home and abroad: in Levinson, S (ed.) (2004), 145–164, p. 158.

36 Parry, J. (2004), 145, citing an "operative" quoted in Priest, Dana and Gellman, Barton (2002) US decries abuse but defends interrogations, *Washington Post*, 26 December, A01.

37 Fon, Antonio Carlos (1979) Descendo aos poroes, *Veja*, 21 February, 64: quoted by Heinz, Wolfgang (1995) The military, torture and human rights: in Crelinsten, R. and Schmid, A. (eds.) (1995), 65–97, p. 83.

38 Tindale, C. (1996), 361; as reported in *Newsweek*, 11 May 1992, 37.

39 Miller, Seamus (2005) Is torture ever morally justified?, *International Journal of Applied Philosophy*, 19, 179–192, 184. On such a view, the distinction between torture as interrogational "tool" and as punishment soon disappears. I am told that his actual position is more nuanced than it appears in writing.

40 Tindale, Christopher (2005) Tragic choices: reaffirming absolutes in the torture debate, *International Journal of Applied Philosophy*, 19, 209–222, p. 210.

41 Levinson, Sanford (2003) The debate on torture, *Dissent*, Summer, unpaginated: available at www.dissentmagazine.org/article/?article=490.

Chapter 2   The Fantasy of the Ticking Bomb Scenario

1   Dershowitz, Alan (2002c) *Why Terrorism Works*, Yale University Press, New Haven and London, 132.
2   Thomson, Judith Jarvis (1985) The trolley problem, *Yale Law Journal*, 94, 1395–1415. The original formulation goes back at least to Foot, Philippa (1967) The problem of abortion and the doctrine of double effect, *Oxford Review*, 5, 5–15 (reprinted in Foot, P. (2002) *Virtues and Vices*, Blackwell, Oxford, 19–32).
3   Dershowitz, A. (2002c), 137.
4   Dershowitz, A. (2002c), 140–1.
5   Davis, Michael (2005) The moral justifiability of torture and other cruel, inhuman, or degrading treatment, *International Journal of Applied Philosophy*, 19, 161–178, p. 170.
6   Dershowitz, A. (2002c), 140.
7   Robin, Corey (2005) Protocols of machismo [a review of Walzer, Michael (2004) *Arguing About War*, Yale University Press, New Haven and London; Hersch, Seymour (2004) *Chain of Command*, Penguin, Harmondsworth; and Levinson, Sanford (ed.) (2004) *Torture: A Collection*, Oxford University Press, Oxford], *London Review of Books*, 19 May, 11–14, pp. 13–14.
8   Elshtain, Jean Bethke (2004) Reflection on the problem of "dirty hands", in Levinson, Sanford (ed.) (2004), 77–89, p. 78. For her objections to legalizing torture, see 83, 87.
9   Robin, C. (2005), 14. Of course, the routinization of *torture* and the *routinization* of torture are both objectionable (hence my chapter three), but Robin is right that the fundamental issue is *torture*.
10 Elshtain, J. B. (2004), 80.
11 Allen, Jonathan (2005) Warrant to torture? A critique of Dershowitz and Levinson, ACDIS Occasional Paper, Program in Arms Control, Disarmament, and International Security, University of Illinois at Urbana-Champaign, 13: available at www.acdis.uiuc.edu.
12 Shue, Henry (1978) Torture, *Philosophy and Public Affairs*, 7, 124–143, p. 141. Reprinted in Levinson, Sanford (ed.) (2004), 47–60.
13 Shue, H. (1978), 141.
14 Shue, H. (1978), 143.
15 Shue, H. (1978), 142.
16 Shue, H. (1978), 143.
17 Flew, Antony (1974) Torture: could the end justify the means?, *Crucible*, January, 19–23, p. 23.
18 Jackson, Richard (2005a) The discursive construction of torture in the war on terrorism: narratives of danger and evil, paper delivered to a conference on The Barbarization of Warfare, University of Wolverhampton, 27–28 June, 16, recently published in Kassimeris, George (ed.) (2006) *Warrior's Dishonour: Barbarity,*

Morality and Torture in Modern Warfare, Ashgate, Aldershot, 141–170; quoting Rose, David (2004) *Guantanamo: America's War on Human Rights*, Faber and Faber, London, 143–145.

19 Quinton, Anthony (1971) Views, *The Listener*, 2 December, 757–758, p. 758.

20 Quinton, A. (1971), 758.

21 Jones, Gary (1980) On the permissibility of torture, *Journal of Medical Ethics*, 6, 11–15.

22 Levin, Michael (1982) The case for torture, *Newsweek*, 7 June, 13: available at www.people.brandeis.edu/~teuber/torture.html.

23 Allhoff, Fritz (2003) Terrorism and torture, *International Journal of Applied Philosophy*, 17, 121–134, p. 129.

24 Walzer, Michael (2003) The United States in the world – just wars and just societies: an interview with Michael Walzer, *Imprints* 7, 4: available at www.eis.bris. ac.uk/~plcdib/imprints/michaelwalzerinterview.html. See also, for example, Hösle, Vittorio (2004) *Morals and Politics*, trans. Rendall, Steven, University of Notre Dame Press, Notre Dame, 434; Sheleff, Leon (1987) *Ultimate Penalties: Capital Punishment, Life Imprisonment, Physical Torture*, Ohio State University Press, Columbus, 304ff.; and Sheleff, L. (2002) The necessity of defence of the truth: on the torturous deliberations about the use of torture, *Bar Ilan Law Studies*, 17, 485–488. Walzer's original argument (1973) is in his Political action: the problem of dirty hands, *Philosophy and Public Affairs*, 2, 160–180, reprinted in Levinson (ed.) (2004), 61–75.

25 Lippman, Matthew (1979) The protection of universal human rights: the problem of torture, *Universal Human Rights* 1, 25–55, p. 29, quoting Ackroyd, Carol, Margolis, Karen, Rosehead, Jonathan and Shallice, Tim (1977) *The Technology of Political Control*, Penguin, Harmondsworth, 231.

26 Crelinsten, Ronald (1995) In their own words: the world of the torturer, in Crelinsten, R. and Schmid, A. (eds.) (1995), 65–97.

27 For a comprehensive survey, see for example Conroy, John (2000) *Unspeakable Acts, Ordinary People: The Dynamics of Torture*, Knopff, New York; for a treatment of the use of torture by America and its allies, see Harbury, Jennifer (2005) *Truth, Torture and the American Way: The History and Consequences of US Involvement in Torture*, Beacon Press, Boston; Danner, Mark (2004b) *Torture and Truth: America, Abu Ghraib, and the War on Terror*, New York Review of Books, New York; and Scheppele, Kim Lane (2005) Hypothetical torture in the "war on terrorism", *Journal of National Security Law and Policy*, 1, 285–340, 335ff. For a British example, see Elkins, Caroline (2005) *Britain's Gulag: The Brutal End of Empire in Kenya*, Jonathan Cape, London (published in the USA as Elkins, C. (2005) *Imperial Reckoning: The Untold Story of Britain's Gulag in Kenya*, Henry Holt, New York).

28 Rose, David (2004), 95.

29 Dershowitz, A. (2002c), 138.

30 Cited in Pachecco, Allegra (1999) *The Case Against Torture in Israel: A Compilation of Petitions, Briefs and Other Documents Submitted to the Israeli High Court of Justice*, The Public Committee Against Torture in Israel, Jerusalem: Abed Al-Rahman Ghanimat and The Public Committee Against Torture vs. The State of

Israel et al. (Bagaatz 7563/97) and Fuad Qur'an and The Public Committee Against Torture in Israel vs. The State of Israel et al. (Bagatz 7628/97), Supplement to Principal Arguments for the Petitioners, Sec. D, para. 2. Available at www.stoptorture.org.il/eng/publications.asp?menu=78submenu=2.

31 Biletzki, Anat (2001) offers an analysis of the Israeli experience in The judicial rhetoric of morality: Israel's High Court of Justice on the legality of torture, unpublished paper: available at www.sss.ias.edu/publications/papers/papernine/pdf.

32 Dershowitz's (2002c, 140) claim, incidentally, that 'There is little doubt that some acts of terrorism – which would have killed many civilians – were prevented' is unreferenced.

33 Dershowitz, A. (2002c), 138.

34 Dershowitz, A. (2002c), 152. As Markus Wagner points out, to take what the French did in Algeria as 'the most extreme example of . . . a hypocritical approach to torture' (Dershowitz, A. (2002c), 152) is to say the least unwarranted, since 'it is important to note that a general amnesty was granted for those crimes committed in the Algerian war'. See Wagner, M. (2003) The justification of torture. Some remarks on Alan M. Dershowitz's *Why Terrorism Works*, 4 *German Law Journal* 5, 1 May, 1–6, p. 2: available at www.germanlawjournal.com/article. php?id=274. Wagner's carefully researched and detailed review is all the more excoriating for its measured tone.

35 Dershowitz, A. (2002c), 137.

36 Dershowitz, A. (2002c), 249, n. 11.

37 Dershowitz, A. (2002c), 137. Wagner (2003) draws attention to the fact that Dershowitz also 'claims that the "United States has prevented many acts of terrorism". However, he fails to cite even one such case.' Note how in his brief consideration of effectiveness, Allhoff also undermines his ticking bomb scenario: '. . . there is no evidence that anyone can resist torture-laden interrogations *indefinitely*' (my emphasis) – Allhoff, F. (2003), 130.

38 Dershowitz, A. (2002c), 144.

39 Dershowitz, A. (2002c), 249, n. 11.

40 Caola, Daniel (2005) letter to *London Review of Books*, 2 June, 4. His comment on Robin's review (n. 7) is admirably trenchant. Cf. Arrigo, Jean Maria (2003), A consequentialist argument against torture interrogation of terrorists, paper given at Joint Services Conference on Professional Ethics, Springfield, Virginia, 30–31 January 2003, 5: available at www.atlas.usafa.af.mil/jscope/JSCOPE03/Arrigo03.html and subsequently published as Arrigo, J. M. (2004) A utilitarian argument against torture interrogation of terrorists, *Science and Engineering Ethics*, 10, 543–572; and Bufacchi, Vittorio and Arrigo, Jean Maria (2006) Tortured reasoning, *Journal of Applied Philosophy* 23, 355–373.

41 Langbein, John (2004) The legal history of torture, in Levinson, S. (ed.) (2004), 93–103, p. 101. For the full version of that history, see Langbein, John (1977) *Torture and the Law of Proof: Europe and England in the Ancien Régime*, Chicago University Press, Chicago. See too Peters, Edwards (1999) *Torture*, University of Pennsylvania Press, Philadelphia, expanded edition, which also contains a very full bibliography of the history of torture.

42 Dershowitz, A. (2002c), 144.

43 Dershowitz, A. (2002c), 249, n. 11.

44 Levinson, Sanford (2003) The debate on torture, *Dissent*, Summer, unpaginated, n. 1; available at www.dissentmagazine.org.

45 He may of course have addressed it elsewhere; or I may have failed to find it.

46 Allen, J. (2005), 10.

47 Roach, Kent (2003) *September 11: Consequences for Canada*, McGill-Queen's University Press, Montreal/Kingston, 101–102; quoted in Plaxton, Michael (2005) Torture warrants, hypocrisy, and supererogation: justifying bright-line rules as if consequences mattered, paper delivered to The Barbarization of Warfare conference, University of Wolverhampton, 27–28 June, 8, recently published in Kassimeris, G. (ed.) (2006), 205–222.

48 Plaxton, M. (2005), 8.

49 A useful summary is to be found in Parry, John and White, Welsh (2002) Interrogating suspected terrorists: should torture be an option?, *University of Pittsburgh Law Review*, 63, 743–766, pp. 754–757.

50 Casebeer, Major (USAF) William (2003) Torture interrogation of terrorists: a theory of exceptions (with notes, cautions, and warnings); available at www. atlas.usafa.af.mil/jscope/JSCOPE03/Casebeer03.html. Or, as Henry Shue puts it, more cautiously, 'one cannot easily draw conclusions for ordinary cases from extraordinary ones, and as situations described become more likely, the conclusion that torture is permissible becomes more debatable'. – Shue (1978), 141–142. Unfortunately, his own position does not take sufficient account of just that sort of point, 'since it offers the retrospective guarantee of success to justify torture (although only in such a case), yet includes the fanatic, whose willingness to die rather than submit would act to undermine that very guarantee of success. This inconsistency may stem from Shue's only half-hearted adoption of the hard case'. – Tindale, Christopher (1996) The logic of torture: a critical examination, *Social Theory and Practice*, 22, 349–374, p. 367. I suspect the confusion arises from Shue's being over-impressed by the 'hard case'.

51 Allen, J. (2005), 9. See also Tindale, Christopher (2005) Tragic choices: reaffirming absolutes in the torture debate, *International Journal of Applied Philosophy*, 19, 209–222, p. 216, and Twining, W. L. and Twining, P. E. (1973) Bentham on torture, *Northern Ireland Legal Quarterly*, 24, 307–356. They say that, for Bentham, the conditions that would have to be satisfied for torture to be justified in a particular case are these: '(1) The evidence in support of the contention that he has the relevant information would satisfy the requirements of evidence for convicting him of an offence. (2) There are reasonable grounds for believing that he is likely to tell the truth if severe torture is threatened, and, if necessary, applied to him. (3) There are reasonable grounds for believing that no other means would have the effect of compelling him to tell the truth. (4) There are reasonable grounds for believing that if the information is obtained quickly, there is a good chance of defusing the bomb before it goes off. (5) There are reasonable grounds for believing that the likely damage to be caused by the bomb will include death of many citizens, the maiming of others, including the infliction of much more severe pain *on others* with much more lasting effect than will be the effect of the

infliction of torture on the person who has been captured. (6) There are reasonable grounds for believing that the torturing will not have consequences (e.g. retaliation by X's friends) which would be worse than the damage likely to result from the bomb going off'. – 346–347. For a good discussion of Bentham's own position see Morgan, Rod (2000) The utilitarian justification of torture: denial, desert and disinformation, *Punishment and Society*, 2, 181–196.

52 Allen, J. (2005), 9.
53 Levinson, S. (2003), unpaginated.
54 Levinson, S. (2003), n. 1.
55 Dershowitz, A. (2002c), 140.
56 Solomon, Alisa (2001) The case against torture, *Village Voice* November 28–December 4, 2; available at www.villagevoice.com/news/0148,fsolomon,30292,1.html.
57 Twining, W. L. and Twining, P. E. (1973), 346.
58 Dershowitz, A. (2002c), 142–143, quoting Bentham, as quoted by Twining and Twining (1973), 347. Their own version of the first condition Bentham has in mind makes just this mistake. But Dershowitz, not least as a lawyer, should surely be alive to it.
59 Dershowitz, A. (2002c), 140.
60 Walzer, M. (1973), 167.
61 Scarry, Elaine (2004) Five errors in the reasoning of Alan Dershowitz, in Levinson, S. (ed.), (2004), 281–299, p. 284. As the reviewer of the final draft pointed out to me, even she makes the mistake of referring to 'us' here, something I had myself overlooked.
62 Trigg, Roger (2004) *Morality Matters*, Blackwell, Oxford, 64.
63 Scarry, E. (2004), 284.
64 Pachecco , A. (1999), sec. F, para. 11a. Cf. 11b, 11c.
65 Arrigo, J. M. (2003), 10.
66 Dershowitz, A. (2002c), 137.
67 Consider the gratuitously silly fantasy of having captured 'one of the terrorists who admits to having planted the bomb, but who smugly refuses to reveal its location' – Jones, Gary (1980) On the permissibility of torture, *Journal of Medical Ethics*, 6, 11–15, p. 13. Even Anthony Quinton (1971), usually a careful thinker, invites us to 'Consider a man caught planting a bomb in a large hospital, which no one dare touch for fear of setting it off' – 758, n. 5. But the knowledge which is a necessary condition of the necessity of torture precludes the relevance of the example: how likely is it that 'no one' – not even the bomb disposal unit – dare touch the bomb? And if it really *were* the case that only this man can defuse the bomb, then it is not for *information* that he would be tortured, but rather to force him to defuse the bomb; and that is quite a different matter.
68 Scarry, E. (2004), 284.
69 Tindale, C. (2005), 365.
70 Biletzki, Anat (2001), 12. See also Lippman, M. (1979), 31–32, for an account of what the UK Parker Committee recommended regarding 'legal regulation and institutionalization of such techniques' (of 'torture and harsh treatment') in response to what British troops were doing in Northern Ireland the late 1960s and early 1970s.

71 Dershowitz, A. (2002c), 150.
72 Dershowitz, A. (2002c), 155.
73 Dershowitz, A. (2002c), 147.
74 Arrigo (2003), 9 (quoting Horne, Alistair (1977) *A Savage War of Peace*, no publisher given, 204–205).
75 Paskins, Barrie (1976) What's wrong with torture?, *British Journal of International Studies* 2 138–148, p. 144.
76 Wagner, M. (2003), 1, 3.
77 For a concise deconstruction of the ticking bomb scenario not unlike my own in this chapter, see Luban, David (2005) Liberalism, torture, and the ticking bomb, *Virginia Law Review*, 91, 1425–1461, pp. 1442ff.

Chapter 3   The Consequences of Normalizing Interrogational Torture

1 From an interview in the *Guardian*, 16 July 1997, quoted by Pachecco, Allegra (1999) *The Case Against Torture in Israel: a compilation of petitions, briefs and other documents submitted to the Israeli High Court of Justice*, the Public Committee Against Torture in Israel, Jerusalem: 'Supplement to Principal Arguments for the Petitioners (Submitted January 11, 1998)', Section D, Paragraph 4: available at www.stoptorture.org.il/eng/publications.asp?menu=7&submenu=2.

2 I discuss the issue of impact on the moral climate in relation to surrogacy agreements, pornography and selling kidneys for transplant in Brecher, Bob (1998) *Getting What You Want? A Critique of Liberal Morality*, Routledge, London, 160–171.

3 See, for example, *British Medical Journal* (1981) 283, Editorial: Dr Leonard Arthur: his trial and its implications, 1340–1341.

4 Dershowitz, Alan (2004a) Tortured reasoning, in Levinson, Sanford (ed.) (2004) *Torture: A Collection*, Oxford University Press, Oxford, 257–280, p. 264. Concerning the impact of his proposal on the moral climate, Dershowitz argues that the present situation, where torture is illegal but both practised and condoned, is not only hypocritical but is also one where far more torture is carried out than would be the case under his proposal. The 'goal' of his 'controversial proposal', he insists, 'was, and remains, to reduce the use of torture to the smallest amount and degree possible, while creating public accountability for its rare use', something he sees as 'not as a compromise with civil liberties but rather as an effort to maximize civil liberties in the face of a realistic likelihood that torture would, in fact, take place below the radar screen of accountability' (259). But, as he argued in *Why Terrorism Works*, 'It does not necessarily follow from this understandable fear of the slippery slope that we can never consider the use of nonlethal infliction of pain, if its use were to be limited by acceptable principles of morality' (147). Admittedly, 'If we create a legal structure for limiting and controlling torture, we compromise our principled opposition to torture in all

circumstances and create a potentially dangerous and expandable situation' (153). Nevertheless, while 'The strongest argument against any resort to torture' is 'that if torture, which has been deemed illegitimate by the civilized world for more than a century, were now to be legitimated – even for limited use in one extraordinary type of situation – such legitimation would constitute an important symbolic setback in the worldwide campaign against human rights abuses', (145) this is offset by the advantages of legalization. This is hardly an adequate discussion. Still, at least Dershowitz addresses the issue. Most academic lawyers favouring interrogational torture seem disinclined to consider these issues at all: an instructive example, for all the detail of his discussion of different forms of utilitarianism, varieties of moral consideration and balances of evil, is Moore, Michael (1989) Torture and the balance of evils, *Israel Law Review* 23, 280–344. See especially 323ff. for what is *not* discussed.

5   Dershowitz, A. (2004a), 266.

6   Dershowitz, A. (2002c) *Why Terrorism Works*, Yale University Press, New Haven and London, 142 and ff.

7   Dershowitz, A. (2002c), 144.

8   Dershowitz, A. (2002c), 146.

9   Dershowitz, A. (2002c), 146.

10 Dershowitz, A. (2002c), 147. He adds, in a later radio interview, only that 'we would not permit that in a democratic country under any circumstances, the torturing of innocent relatives' – 'The US is now currently engaged in torturing people', Radio Netherlands 04/18/03: available at www. informationclearinghouse.info/article3044.htm.

11 Biletzki, Anat (2001) The judicial rhetoric of morality: Israel's High Court of Justice on the legality of torture, unpublished paper, 9: available at www.sss.ias. edu/publications/papers/papernine/pdf. Cf. Plaxton, Michael (2005) Torture warrants, hypocrisy and supererogation: justifying bright-line rules as if consequences mattered, paper delivered at a conference on the Barbarization of Warfare, University of Wolverhampton, 27–28 June, 17ff.: recently published in Kassimeris, G. (ed.) (2006) *The Warrior's Dishonour: Barbarity, Morality and Torture in Modern Warfare*, Ashgate, Aldershot, 205–222.

12 Kreimer, Seth (2003) Too close to the rack and screw, *University of Pennsylvania Journal of Constitutional Law*, 6, 278–325, p. 306. Cf. Human Rights Watch (1992) Israeli interrogation methods under fire after death of detained Palestinian, *Human Rights Watch* 4: available at www.hrw.org/reports/1992/israel/.

13 Dershowitz, A. (2002c), 147.

14 Dershowitz, A. (2004b) The torture warrant: a response to Professor Strauss, *New York Law School Legal Review*, 48, 275–294, p. 291. The quotation is from Strauss, Marcy (2004) Torture, *New York Law School Law Review*, 48, 201–274, p. 274 (Dershowitz's own cited pagination is a misprint).

15 But even then, he is surely wrong to castigate Elaine Scarry for 'erroneously characteriz(ing) (his) view' (2004a, 274) when she says that he 'believes that in such a situation [the ticking bomb scenario] it would be permissible to torture if one first obtained a judicial or executive warrant' (Scarry, Elaine (2004) Five errors in the reasoning of Alan Dershowitz, in Levinson, S. (ed.) (2004), 281–290,

p. 281). For in light of his own confusions, omissions and lack of explicitness, such a conclusion is hardly unreasonable. Not only that: an argument that interrogational torture should be legalized *simply and solely* because it is the best, or the only, way *of controlling torture* is so odd that it would need to be made very clear that that is indeed the argument. And while Dershowitz does so in his later essay, he does not do so in *Why Terrorism Works*. So it is hardly any wonder that when he says in 'Tortured reasoning' that he is 'against torture as a *normative* matter', his critics should be taken aback. For *unlike* in the anti-abortion and anti-drug cases mentioned above, where *opponents* of the practice nonetheless support its legalization, Dershowitz's argument in *Why Terrorism Works* gives every appearance of being based on two convictions: that interrogational torture in the ticking bomb scenario is morally justified and that its being legalized would limit torture. Why otherwise the attempt to present it as necessary, as "the lesser evil", on the grounds that the "terrorist" has information needed to avoid imminent catastrophe? Furthermore, this second argument is by far the more prominent one in the book. If Dershowitz's *sole* reason for advocating the legalization of interrogational torture in ticking bomb circumstances (given that it is being used and the great majority of people 'believe that torture would actually be used in such a case' (150)) were that it would limit the torture that goes on anyway, then the "avoiding catastrophe" argument would be secondary. Nor (for example) would Dershowitz's claim that 'It is impossible to avoid the difficult moral dilemma of choosing among evils by denying the empirical reality that torture *sometimes* works, even if it does not always work' (137) be to the point. Rather, he would have to have written something like this: 'It is impossible to avoid the difficult moral dilemma of choosing among evils by denying the empirical reality that torture is best controlled and limited by legalizing it in the ticking bomb scenario . . .'; and to have added, perhaps, that its 'sometimes' working is just as well, since otherwise the proposal that it be legalized in order so far as possible to put a stop to torture would appear wildly implausible. But he did not.

16 Dershowitz, A. (2004a), 260–262.

17 Dershowitz, A. (2004a), 271–272.

18 Dershowitz, A. (2002c), 158.

19 Dershowitz, A. (2002c), 162.

20 Dershowitz, A. (2002c), 158. The quotation is from Langbein, John (1977) *Torture and the Law of Proof*, Chicago University Press, Chicago, 139. Cf. Allen, Jonathan (2005) Warrant to torture? A critique of Dershowitz and Levinson, ACDIS Occasional Paper, Program in Arms Control, Disarmament, and International Security, University of Illinois at Urbana-Champaign, 10–11: available at www.acdis. uiuc.edu. See Waldron, Jeremy (2005) Torture and positive law: jurisprudence for the White House, *Columbia Law Review*, 105, 1681–1750, pp. 1739–1740, n. 250, on how Dershowitz misrepresents Langbein.

21 Dershowitz, A. (2002c), 158.

22 Kremnitzer, Mordecai and Segev, Re'em (2000) The legality of interrogational torture: a question of proper authorization or a substantive moral issue?, *Israel Law Review*, 34, 2000, 509–559, p. 513. No serious commentator denies this. See also Felner, Eitan (2005) Torture and terrorism: painful lessons from Israel, in

Roth, Ken and Worden, Minky (eds.) (2005) *Torture*, New Press and Human Rights Watch, New York, 28–43.

23   Ziv, Hadas (undated) *Physicians and torture – the case of Israel*, Physicians for Human Rights – Israel, Introduction (my emphasis): available at www.hdip. org/Health&the-uprising-1.htm.

24   B'Tselem (2000) Position Paper on Legislation Allowing the use of Physical Force and Mental Coercion in Interrogations by the General Security Service, 3: available at www.btselem.org.

25   B'Tselem (2000), 4.

26   Dershowitz, A. (2002c), 157ff. For detailed accounts of the historical picture, see Langbein, J. (1977); Peters, Edward (1999) *Torture*, University of Pennsylvania Press, Philadelphia, expanded edition, 40–102; and Waldron, Jeremy (2005), 1718ff.

27   Dershowitz, A. (2002c), 158–159.

28   Dershowitz, A. (2002c), 155.

29   Twining, W. L. and Twining, P. E. (1973) Bentham on torture, *Northern Ireland Legal Quarterly*, 307–356, pp. 348–349; for their utilitarian arguments against legalization, see 352–353. Cf. Twining, W. (1978) Torture and philosophy, *Proceedings of the Aristotelian Society (Supplement)*, 52, 143–168, p. 147, where he emphasizes the distinction 'between an isolated act and an institutionalized practice of torturing'.

30   Dershowitz, A. (2002c), 153. See Kremnitzer, M. and Segev, R. (2000), 534, for a particularly incisive statement of this position.

31   Dershowitz, A. (2002c), 154.

32   My thanks to Vanessa Munro for serendipitously suggesting the example to me.

33   This might go some way towards explaining his otherwise somewhat paradoxical 'personal hope [is] that no torture warrant would ever be issued, because the criteria for obtaining one would be so limited and rigorous' – Dershowitz, A. (2002a) letter to the editor, *San Francisco Chronicle* 28 January, B4: quoted in Parry, John and White, Welsh (2002) Interrogating suspected terrorists: should torture be an option?, *University of Pittsburgh Law Review*, 63, 743–766, p. 747, n. 14.

34   Peters, E. (1999), 140, quoting Vidal-Naquet, Pierre (1963) *Torture: Cancer of Democracy: France and Algeria 1954–62*, Penguin, Harmondsworth.

35   Kreimer, S. (2003), 319.

36   Amnesty International (1984) *Torture in the Eighties*, Amnesty International, London, 7. For an excellent contemporary summary of how the institutionalization of interrogational torture may be expected to impact upon society see Tindale, Christopher (2005) Tragic choices: reaffirming absolutes in the torture debate, *International Journal of Applied Philosophy*, 19, 209–222, pp. 217–219.

37   Felner, E. (2005), 42–43.

38   Dershowitz, A. (2002c), 249, n. 11.

39   Waldron, J. (2005), 1717. See also Amnesty International (2004) *United States of America: Human Dignity Denied – Torture and Accountability in the "War on Terror"*, Part One: available at www.amnesty.org/library/index/engamr511452004.

40 As we have seen, in his latest book (at time of writing), Dershowitz advocates legalizing "pre-emptive strikes" in certain situations: see Dershowitz, Alan (2006) *Preemption: A Knife That Cuts Both Ways*, W. W. Norton, New York.

41 See, for example, many of the essays in Crelinsten, R. and Schmid, A. (eds.) (1995) *The Politics of Pain: Torturers and their Masters*, Westview Press, Oxford; Amnesty International (2004); and Harbury, Jennifer (2005) *Truth, Torture, and the American Way: The History and Consequences of US Involvement in Torture*, Beacon Press, Boston. For an excellent analysis of how the torture and abuse of innocent Iraqis at Abu Ghraib exemplifies the internal logic of torture once the practice is permitted (however "informally", as by the Bush administration), see Danner, Mark (2004a) The logic of torture, in Danner, M. (2004b) *Torture and Truth: America, Abu Ghraib, and the War on Terror*, New York Review of Books, New York, 10–25.

42 Kremnitzer, M. and Segev, R. (2000), 549.

43 With thanks to Jacob Strutt.

44 *Economist* (2003) Editorial, Is torture ever justified?, 9 January, 10–11.

45 Kreimer, S. (2003), 291, citing 'Brief for the Petitioner at 27 n.8, Chavez v. Martinez, 123 S. Ct. 1994 (2003) (No. 01–1444) . . .' – n. 44 . That 'the Court pointedly declined these invitations' (ibid.) is reassuring: but for how long? For a thoughtful and sensitive account of just such a genuine case in Germany, see Schroeder, Doris (2006) A child's life or a "little bit of torture"? State-sanctioned violence and dignity, *Cambridge Quarterly of Health Care Ethics*, 188–201. I shall return to this in chapter four.

46 B'Tselem (2000).

47 Human Rights Watch (1992) *Israeli interrogation methods under fire after death of detained Palestinian*, vol. 4, issue 6: available at www.hrw.org/reports/1992/Israel. See also Pachecco, A. (1999), Kremnitzer, M. and Segev, R. (2000) and Biletzki, A. (2001); and compare Amnesty International (1984).

48 Pokempner, D. (2005) Command responsibility for torture, in Roth, K. and Worden, M. (eds.) (2005), 167.

49 For details, see Biletzki, A. (2001), 8. The Israeli Supreme Court's 1999 'Judgement on the interrogation methods applied by the GSS' clearly and unambiguously admits this. It states, for example, that 'the GSS also investigates those suspected of hostile terrorist activities. The purpose of these interrogations is, *among others*, to gather information regarding terrorists and their organizing methods for the purpose of thwarting and preventing them from carrying out these terrorist attacks.' – 3, my emphasis. The judgement is available at www. derechos.org/human-rights/mena/doc/torture.html. Biletzki explores in detail in this paper what appear to him and to others its ambiguities regarding 'Physical Means and the "Necessity" Defence' (17 ff.), for all that it was popularly taken to have stopped torture *tout court*. A more optimistic interpretation is offered by May, Larry (2005) Torturing detainees during interrogation, *International Journal of Applied Philosophy*, 19, 193–208, pp. 198–201. See also Dershowitz, A. (2004a), 259–264 and (2002c), 140; and Ziv, H. (undated).

50 Biletzki, A. (2001), 9. Cf. Allen, J. (2005), and Parry, J. and White, W. (2002), 757–760.

51 For an interesting defence of "legal hypocrisy" based on arguments that legalization would be disastrous, see Kadish, Sanford (1989) Torture, the state and the individual, *Israel Law Review*, 23, 345–356, esp. 352–356.

52 See Amnesty International (1984), 6–8.

53 Interview cited by Crelinsten, Ronald (1995) In their own words: the world of the torturer, in Crelinsten, R. and Schmid, A. (eds.) (1995), 35–64, p. 51.

54 Dershowitz, A. (2002c), 142.

55 Gonzales, Alberto (2002) Draft memorandum for the President from Alberto R. Gonzales: Decision re application of the Geneva Convention on prisoners of war to the conflict with Al Qaeda and the Taliban, 25 January: available at www.msnbc.msn.com/id/4999148/site/newsweek.

56 Kreimer, S. (2003), 319.

57 Parry, J. and White, W. (2002), 762: see 763 for a summary of further undesirable practical consequences that Parry and White think likely.

58 Peters, E. (1999), 57.

59 Luban, David (2005) Liberalism, torture, and the ticking bomb, *Virginia Law Review*, 91, 1425–1461, p. 1452.

60 See Waldron, J. (2005), for a definitive analysis of the infamous memoranda.

61 Luban, D. (2005), 1453; see also 1452–1460.

62 Parry, J. and White, W. (2002), 762.

63 Plaxton, M. (2005), 7.

64 Kreimer, S. (2003), 322.

65 *Economist* (2003), 11. Cf. Crelinsten, R. (1995), 36–37.

66 Biletzki, A. (2001), 9–10.

67 Danner, M. (2004b), 76.

68 Posner, Richard (2004) Torture, terrorism and interrogation, in Levinson (ed.) (2004), 291–298, p. 295. For a similar, but empirically far better informed, defence of illegal torture, see Miller, Seumas (2005) Is torture ever morally justifiable?, *International Journal of Applied Philosophy*, 19, 179–192. Nonetheless, he fails to examine his own assumptions regarding both the nature of torture (see chapter four) and the impact on the moral climate of "one-off", illegal, torture.

69 Posner, R. (2004), 296.

70 Waldron, J. (2005), 1726, 1727. The quotation is from Arendt, Hannah (1973, new ed.) *The Origins of Totalitarianism*, Harcourt Brace Jovanovich, New York, 441. Compare Michael Ignatieff's view that 'torture, when committed by a state, expresses the state's ultimate view that human beings are expendable. This view is antithetical to the spirit of any constitutional society whose raison d'etre is the control of violence and coercion in the name of human dignity and freedom': Ignatieff, Michael (2004) *The Lesser Evil: Political Ethics in an Age of Terror*, Princeton University Press, Princeton, 8–9.

71 See also Bloom, Mia (2005) *Dying to Kill: The Allure of Suicide Terror*, Columbia University Press, New York.

72 Rose, David (2004) *Guantanamo: America's War on Human Rights*, Faber and Faber, London, 34.
73 *Independent* (2006) Beckett admits Guantanamo Bay camp should be shut down, 13 October: available at www.news.independent.co.uk/uk/politics/article/1868066.ece.
74 Crelinsten, R. (1995), 36. The quotations are from a Khmer Rouge torture manual.
75 Crelinsten, R. (1995), 51–54.
76 Crelinsten, R. (1995), 54. Cf. Arrigo, Jean Maria (2003), A consequentialist argument against torture interrogation of terrorists, paper given at Joint Services Conference on Professional Ethics, Springfield, Virginia, 30–31 January 2003, 8: available at www.atlas.usafa.af.mil/jscope/JSCOPE03/Arrigo03.html, and subsequently published as Arrigo, J. (2004) A utilitarian argument against torture interrogation of terrorists, *Science and Engineering Ethics*, 10, 543–572; and Rose, D. (2004), ch. 3, *passim*.
77 Amnesty International (1984), 7. For examples of how this works out in practice, see Pachecco, A. (1999).
78 Žižek, Slavoj (2006) The depraved heroes of 24 are the Himmlers of Hollywood, *Guardian* 10 January, 27. Cf. Waldron, J. (2005), 1715, n. 151.
79 Langguth, A. L. (1978) *Hidden Terrors: The Truth about US Police Operations in Latin America*, Pantheon, New York, 201; quoted by Crelinsten, R. (1995), 56.
80 Crelinsten, R. (1995), 46–51.
81 Crelinsten, R. (1995), 49. For a disturbingly graphic set of details of the training required, based on interviews with members of the Greek junta after its collapse, see Haritos-Fatouros, Mika (1995) The official torturer, in Crelinsten, R. and Schmid, A. (eds.) (1995), 129–146.
82 Cosculluela, Manuel Hevia (1978) *Pasaporte 11333: ocho años con la CIA*, Editorial de Sciencias Social, Havana, 284: quoted by Harbury, Janet (2005), 96.
83 Rose, D. (2004), 72, 73.
84 *New Statesman* (2003) 17 February, 22–25.
85 Peters, E. (1999), 57.
86 Peters, E. (1999), 125.
87 Ziv, H. (undated), 9.
88 Bloche, M. Gregg and Marks, Jonathan H. (2005) Doctors and interrogators at Guantanamo Bay, *New England Journal of Medicine*, 353, 6–8, p. 6. Cf. Rose, D. (2004) and Danner, M. (2004b).
89 Bloche, M. G. and Marks, J. H. (2005), 8.
90 For a defence of professional prohibition, see Heijder, Alfred and van Geuns, Herman (1976) *Professional Code of Ethics*, Amnesty International Publications, London; and for the difficulties that arise 'in operationalizing professional codes of conduct', see Lippman, Matthew (1979) The protection of universal human rights: the problem of torture, *Universal Human Rights*, 1, 25–55, pp. 46ff. For a detailed case study focusing on Israel (and which also has a good deal of material on the general issue of torture), see Gordon, Neve and Marton, Ruchama (1995) *Torture: Human Rights, Medical Ethics and the Case of Israel*, Zed Books, London.

91 Ziv, H. (undated), 8; see also 10.
92 See Arrigo, J. M. (2003), 3–7.
93 Ziv, H. (undated), 15. For a communitarian defence of doctors' duty to assist with torture in non-liberal but "decent" societies, just as doctors in "Islamic" societies have a duty to assist with amputation – in both cases because the individual does not come first – see Gross, M. (2004) Doctors in the decent society: torture, ill-treatment and civic duty, *Bioethics*, 18, 181–203. Its extraordinarily insouciant assumptions about "other" societies are typical of the genre.
94 Bloche, M. G. and Marks, J. H. (2005), 7.
95 For example, Shue, Henry (1978) Torture, *Philosophy and Public Affairs*, 7, 124–143, p. 141. Reprinted in Levinson (ed.) (2004), 47–60. A notable exception is Barrie Paskins: Paskins, Barrie (1976) What's wrong with torture?, *British Journal of International Studies*, 2, 138–148, p. 144. See also Paskins, Barrie (1978) Reply (to Twining (1978)) *Proceedings of the Aristotelian Society (Supplement)* 52, 168–178, p. 178.
96 Posner, Richard (2004), Torture, terrorism and interrogation, in Levinson, S. (ed.) (2004), 291–298, p. 295.
97 Kooijmans, Pieter (1995) Torturers and their masters, in Crelinsten, R. and Schmid A. (eds.) (1995), 13–18, p. 13, citing 'a document that I received in October 1991. It contains an elaborate description of the torture methods practiced in a country which has become notorious for the widespread use of torture. I do not know whether the document is genuine or fake.' – 14. I think that Kooijmans' decision to quote from it nonetheless – in light of how closely it corresponds to all too many genuine reports – justifies my own use of the passage.
98 Dershowitz, A. (2002c), 150.

Chapter 4   Torture, Death and Philosophy

1 Tindale, Christopher (1996) The logic of torture, *Social Theory and Practice* 22, 349–374, p. 355.
2 Paskins, Barrie (1976) What's wrong with torture?, *British Journal of International Studies*, 2, 138–148, p. 138.
3 Cover, Robert (1986) Violence and the word, *Yale Law Journal*, 95, 1601–1628, p. 1602. On the purpose of torture, see also Crelinsten, Ronald (1995) In their own words, in Crelinsten, Ronald and Schmid, Alex (eds.) (1995) *The Politics of Pain: Torturers and their Masters*, Westview Press, Boulder, 35–64, pp. 37ff.
4 Davis, Michael (2005) The moral justifiability of torture and other cruel, inhuman, or degrading treatment, *International Journal of Applied Philosophy*, 19, 161–178, p. 165. See 165–167 for how torture is different from every other form of imposing suffering, including, and especially, punishment; and compare Luban, David (2005) Liberalism, torture, and the ticking bomb, *Virginia Law Review*, 91, 1425–1461, pp. 1430–1433.
5 Thus, for example, someone in a persistent vegetative state from which they will never emerge ceases at some point to be a person; they have permanently ceased

to be able to act. A human being born without a brain will never become a person; they will never be able to act. The claim that it is our capacity to act which makes us persons, while it is too large to defend here, is I think the best foundation of the wider and more detailed argument about why torture is uniquely awful that is required fully to justify what I outline here.

6 Améry, Jean (1980) Torture, in Améry, J. (1980) *At the Mind's Limit*, trans. Rosenfeld, S. and S., Indiana University Press, Bloomington, 21–40, p. 33. Cf. Crelinsten, Ronald and Genefke, Inge (2004) Torture: weapon against democracy, in Coates, Ken (ed.) (2004) *Dark Times*, Spokesman Books, Nottingham, 27–31.

7 Dershowitz, Alan (2002c) *Why Terrorism Works*, Yale University Press, New Haven and London, 159.

8 Améry, J. (1980), 22.

9 Améry, J. (1980), 32.

10 Améry, J. (1980), 33. Cf. Crelinsten (1995), 41: 'It has often been reported that screams of torture victims no longer sound human. The irony is that, to the torturer, this only reinforces their dehumanization. One Chilean victim, speaking of her own screams, recalled: "It's much worse than a howl. The sound coming from within is just terrible. It's the worst sound I've ever heard."' The quotation is from a BBC film in the Everyman series: *Called to Account*, 1989. In this context, consider David Sussman's insight that 'Following Elaine Scarry [(1985) *The Body In Pain*, Oxford University Press, New York, 45–51], we might construe pain as something like the "voice" of the body. The comparison to language is illuminating. In many respects, pain is like a sensation, but a sensation that seems to have a kind of immediate significance in which the agent already finds his attention and will to be invested. Normally, one cannot adopt a purely contemplative attitude toward one's own pain. In these respects, feeling pain resembles hearing the utterance of a meaningful sentence. I cannot hear a minimally grammatical English sentence as just noise . . . .' Sussman, Donald (2005) What's wrong with torture?, *Philosophy and Public Affairs*, 33, 1–33, p. 20.

11 Améry, J. (1980), 36.

12 Améry, J. (1980), 27.

13 Améry, J. (1980), 28.

14 Améry, J. (1980), 29.

15 Améry, J. (1980), 40.

16 The phrase is Mark Devenney's; and I am indebted to him for much of the analysis of this idea that follows.

17 Dershowitz, A. (2002c), 144. See also Levin, Michael (1982) The case for torture, *Newsweek*, 7 June, 13: available at www.people.brandeis.edu/~teuber/torture.html.

18 Dershowitz, A. (2002c), 148; and cf. 155. Levinson, however, is clear that the analogy with the death penalty is misplaced: see Levinson, Sanford (2003) The debate on torture, *Dissent*, Summer: available at www.dissentmagazine.org. For comment, see Allen, Jonathan (2005) Warrant to torture? A critique of Dershowitz and Levinson, ACDIS Occasional Paper, Program in Arms Control, Disarmament, and International Security, University of Illinois at Urbana-Champaign, 4, 8: available at www.acdis.uiuc.edu.

19 Dershowitz, A. (2002c), 144.
20 Miller, Seamus (2005) Is torture ever morally justified?, *International Journal of Applied Philosophy*, 19, 179–192, p. 180.
21 I argue against this view in Brecher, Bob (1998) *Getting What You Want? A Critique of Liberal Morality*, Routledge, London.
22 Davis, M. (2005), 165.
23 The assumption has a considerable pedigree: see, for example, Machan, Tibor (1991) Exploring extreme violence (torture), *Journal of Social Philosophy*, 19, 92–97. It is of course connected with the underlying assumption that what matters most to those western thinkers imbued with a liberal/free-market conception of human life and values must matter most to everyone. But it does not. Nor should it.
24 Dershowitz, A. (2002c), 159 (my emphasis).
25 Wiesel, Elie (1981) *Night*, Penguin, Harmondsworth.
26 Kertész, Istvan (2006) *Fateless*, Vintage, London.
27 Dorfman, Ariel (2004) foreword to Levinson, Sanford (ed.) (2004) *Torture: A Collection*, Oxford University Press, Oxford, 3–18, p. 17.
28 Posner, Richard (2004) Torture, terrorism, and interrogation, in Levinson, S. (ed.) (2004), 291–298. p. 295.
29 Miller, S. (2005), 182.
30 Waldron, Jeremy (2005) Torture and positive law: jurisprudence for the White House, *Columbia Law Review*, 105, 1681–1750, p. 1703.
31 Luban, David (2005), 1436. As Luban argues, the ticking bomb scenario 'serves a (second) rhetorical goal', by making 'us see the torturer in a different light'. – p. 1441.
32 Klein, Naomi (2005) The true purpose of torture, the *Guardian*, 14 May, 3: available at www.guardian.co.uk/comment/story/0,,1483801,00.html.
33 See Le Guin, Ursula (2000) The ones who walk away from Omelas, in her *The Wind's Twelve Quarters*, new edition, Gollancz, London.
34 Zamir, Itzhak (1989) Human rights and national security, *Israel Law Review*, 23, 375–406, p. 380; cited by Strauss, Marcy (2004), Torture, *New York Law School Law Review*, 48, 201–274, p. 257.
35 Luban, D. (2005). Cf. Parry, John (2005) The shape of modern torture: extraordinary rendition and ghost detainees, *Melbourne Journal of International Law*, 6, 516–533.
36 See Waldron, J. (2005) for an excellent account of the current international legal state of affairs, including the business of "outsourcing", and with a comprehensive bibliography; see also Pollard, Matt (2005) The absolute and comprehensive prohibition of torture and other cruel, inhuman or degrading treatment or punishment, Swedish Forum on Human Rights, Stockholm 16–17 November, available at www.apt.ch/un/TortureProhibition_SFHR.pdf.
37 Jackson, Richard (2005b) *Writing the War on Terrorism: Language, Politics and Counter-terrorism*, Manchester University Press, Manchester.
38 I say more about this in Brecher, B. (2004) Do intellectuals have a special public responsibility?, in Aiken, Will and Haldane, John (eds.) (2004) *Philosophy and*

its Public Role, Imprint Academic: St Andrews Studies in Philosophy and Public Affairs, Exeter Aiken, 25–38.

39 Schroeder, Doris (2006) A child's life or a "little bit of torture"? State-sanctioned violence and dignity, *Cambridge Quarterly of Healthcare Ethics*, 15, 188–201, p. 188.

40 Schroeder, D. (2006), 189; and see also her conclusion.

41 Ignatieff, Michael (2005) Moral prohibition at a price, in Roth, Ken and Worden, Minky (eds.) (2005) *Torture*, New Press and Human Rights Watch, New York, 18–27, p. 27.

Bibliography

Ackroyd, Carol, Margolis, Karen, Rosehead, Jonathan and Shallice, Tim (1977) *The Technology of Political Control*, Penguin, Harmondsworth.

Aiken, Will and Haldane, John (eds.) (2004) *Philosophy and its Public Role*, Imprint Academic: St Andrews Studies in Philosophy and Public Affairs, Exeter.

Allen, Jonathan (2005) Warrant to torture? A critique of Dershowitz and Levinson, ACDIS Occasional Paper, Program in Arms Control, Disarmament, and International Security, University of Illinois at Urbana-Champaign, 13: available at www. acdis.uiuc.edu.

Allhoff, Fritz (2003) Terrorism and torture, *International Journal of Applied Philosophy*, 17, 121–134.

Améry, Jean (1980) *At the Mind's Limit*, trans. Rosenfeld, S. and S., Indiana University Press, Bloomington.

Améry, Jean (1980) Torture, in Améry, J. (1980), 21–40.

Amnesty International (1984) *Torture in the Eighties*, Amnesty International, London.

Amnesty International (2004) *United States of America: Human Dignity Denied – Torture and Accountability in the "War on Terror"*: available at www.amnesty.org/library/index/engamr511452004.

Arendt, Hannah (1973, new edn.) *The Origins of Totalitarianism*, Harcourt Brace Jovanovich, New York.

Arrigo, Jean Maria (2003) A consequentialist argument against torture interrogation of terrorists, paper given at Joint Services Conference on Professional Ethics, Springfield, Virginia, 30–31 January, 5: available at www.atlas.usafa.af.mil/jscope/JSCOPE03/Arrigo03.html.

Arrigo, Jean Maria (2004) A utilitarian argument against torture interrogation of terrorists, *Science and Engineering Ethics*, 10, 543–572.

Bagaric, Mirko and Clarke, Julie (2005) Not enough official torture in the world? The circumstances in which torture is morally justifiable, *University of San Francisco Law Review*, 39, 581–616.

Bentham, Jeremy (no date) Of torture, Bentham MSS Box 46, 63–70; 56–62.

Biletzki, Anat (2001) The judicial rhetoric of morality: Israel's High Court of Justice on the legality of torture: unpublished paper, available at www.sss.ias. edu/publications/papers/papernine/pdf.

Bloche, M. Gregg and Marks, Jonathan H. (2005) Doctors and interrogators at Guantanamo Bay, *New England Journal of Medicine*, 353, 6–8.

Bloom, Mia (2005) *Dying to Kill: The Allure of Suicide Terror*, Columbia University Press, New York.

Brecher, Bob (1998) *Getting What You Want? A Critique of Liberal Morality*, Routledge, London.

Brecher, Bob (2004) Do intellectuals have a special public responsibility?, in Aiken, W. and Haldane, J. (eds.) (2004), 25–38.

British Medical Journal (1981) 283, Editorial: Dr Leonard Arthur: his trial and its implications, 1340–1341.

B'Tselem (2000) Position Paper on Legislation Allowing the use of Physical Force and Mental Coercion in Interrogations by the General Security Service: available at www.btselem.org.

Bufacchi, Vittorio and Arrigo, Jean Maria (2006) Tortured reasoning, *Journal of Applied Philosophy*, 23, 355–373.

Bybee, Jay S. (2002) Memorandum for Alberto R. Gonzales, Counsel to the President, re: Standards of Conduct for Interrogation under 18 U.S.C. (1 August): in Danner, M. (2004b), 115–166.

Caola, Daniel (2005) Letter to *London Review of Books*, 2 June, 4.

Casebeer, Major (USAF) William (2003) Torture interrogation of terrorists: a theory of exceptions (with notes, cautions, and warnings): available at www.atlas.usafa. af.mil/jscope/JSCOPE03/Casebeer03.html.

Coates, Ken (ed.) (2004) *Dark Times*, Spokesman Books, Nottingham.

Conroy, John (2000) *Unspeakable Acts, Ordinary People: The Dynamics of Torture*, Knopff, New York.

Cosculluela, Manuel Hevia (1978) *Pasaporte 11333: ocho años con la CIA*, Editorial de Sciencias Social, Havana.

Cover, Robert (1986) Violence and the word, *Yale Law Journal*, 95, 1601–1628.

Crelinsten, Ronald (1995) In their own words: the world of the torturer, in Crelinsten, R. and Schmid, A. (eds.) (1995), 65–97.

Crelinsten, Ronald and Schmid, Alex (eds.) (1995) *The Politics of Pain: Torturers and their Masters*, Westview Press, Boulder.

Crelinsten, Ronald and Genefke, Inge (2004) Torture: weapon against democracy, in Coates, Ken (ed.) (2004) Dark Times, Spokesman Books, Nottingham, 27–31.

Danner, Mark (2004a) The logic of torture, in Danner, M. (2004b), 10–25.

Danner, Mark (2004b) *Torture and Truth: America, Abu Ghraib, and the War on Terror*, New York Review of Books, New York.

Davis, Michael (2005) The moral justifiability of torture and other cruel, inhuman, or degrading treatment, *International Journal of Applied Philosophy*, 19, 161–178.

Dershowitz, Alan (1989) Is it necessary to apply "physical pressure" to terrorists – and to lie about it?, *Israel Law Review* 23, 192–200.

Dershowitz, Alan (2001) Is there a torturous road to justice?, 8 November: available at www.groups-beta.google.com/group/alt.impeach.bush/msg/814527 884aa6c904.

Dershowitz, Alan (2002a) Letter to the editor, *San Francisco Chronicle*, 28 January, B4.

Dershowitz, Alan (2002b) *Shouting Fire: Civil Liberties in a Turbulent Age*, Little Brown, New York.

Dershowitz, Alan (2002c) *Why Terrorism Works*, Yale University Press, New Haven and London.

Dershowitz, Alan (2003) The US is now currently engaged in torturing people, Radio Netherlands 04/18/03: available at www.informationclearinghouse.info/article3044. htm.

Dershowitz, Alan (2004a) Tortured reasoning, in Levinson, S. (ed.) (2004), 257–280.

Dershowitz, Alan (2004b) The torture warrant: a response to Professor Strauss, *New York Law School Legal Review*, 48, 275–294.

Dershowitz, Alan (2004c) When torture is the least evil of terrible options, *Times Higher Education Supplement*, 11 June, 20–21.

Dershowitz, Alan (2006a) *Preemption: A Knife That Cuts Both Ways*, Norton, New York.

Dershowitz, Alan (2006b) Should we fight terror with torture?, *Independent*, 3 July (unpaginated): available at www.independent.co.uk.

Dorfman, Ariel (2004) Foreword to Levinson, S. (ed.) (2004), 3–18.

Economist (2003) Editorial, Is torture ever justified?, 9 January, 10–11.

Elkins, Caroline (2005) *Britain's Gulag: The Brutal End of Empire in Kenya*, Jonathan Cape, London. Published in the USA as Elkins, C. (2005) *Imperial Reckoning: The Untold Story of Britain's Gulag in Kenya*, Henry Holt, New York.

Elshtain, Jean Bethke (2004) Reflection on the problem of "dirty hands", in Levinson, S. (ed.) (2004), 77–89.

Evans, Malcolm (2002) Getting to grips with torture, *International and Comparative Law Quarterly*, 51, 365–383.

Felner, Eitan (2005) Torture and terrorism: painful lessons from Israel, in Roth, K. and Worden, M. (eds.) (2005), 28–43.

Flew, Antony (1974) Torture: could the end justify the means?, *Crucible*, January, 19–23.

Fon, Antonio Carlos (1979) Descendo aos poroes, *Veja*, 21 February, 64.

Foot, Philippa (1967) The problem of abortion and the doctrine of double effect, *Oxford Review*, 5, 5–15. Reprinted in Foot, P. (2002) *Virtues and Vices*, Blackwell, Oxford, 19–32.

Gearty, Conor (2005) Legitimizing torture – with a little help from our friends, *Index on Censorship 1/05: Torture – a user's manual*: available at www.indexonline. org/en/news/articles/2005/1/international-legitimising-torture-with-a-li.shtml.

Gonzales, Alberto (2002) Draft memorandum for the President from Alberto R. Gonzales: Decision re application of the Geneva Convention on prisoners of war to the conflict with Al Qaeda and the Taliban, 25 January: available at www.msnbc. msn.com/id/4999148/site/newsweek.

Gonzales, Alberto et al. (2004) Press briefing by White House Counsel Judge Alberto Gonzales, DOD General Counsel William Haynes, DOD Deputy General Counsel Danile Dell'Orto and Army Deputy Chief of Staff for Intelligence General Keith Alexander, 22 June: available at www.whitehouse.gov/news/releases/2004/06/20040622-14.html.

Gordon, Neve and Marton, Ruchama (1995) *Torture: Human Rights, Medical Ethics and the Case of Israel*, Zed Books, London.

Gray, John (2003) A modest proposal: for preventing torturers in liberal democracies from being abused, and for recognizing their benefit to the public, *New Statesman*, 17 February, 22–25.

Greenberg, Karen and Dratel, Joshua (eds.) (2005) *The Torture Papers*, Cambridge University Press, Cambridge.

Grey, Stephen and Cobain, Ian (2006) From logistics to turning a blind eye: Europe's role in terror abduction, *Guardian*, 7 June: available at www.guardian.co.uk.

Gross, M. (2004) Doctors in the decent society: torture, ill-treatment and civic duty, *Bioethics*, 18, 181–203.

Harbury, Jennifer (2005) *Truth, Torture, and the American Way: The History and Consequences of US Involvement in Torture*, Beacon Press, Boston.

Haritos-Fatouros, Mika (1995) The official torturer, in Crelinsten, R. and Schmid, A. (eds.) (1995), 129–146.

Heijder, Alfred and van Geuns, Herman (1976) *Professional Code of Ethics*, Amnesty International Publications, London.

Heinz, Wolfgang (1995) The military, torture and human rights, in Crelinsten, R. and Schmid, A. (eds.) (1995), 65–97.

Hösle, Vittorio (2004) *Morals and Politics*, trans. Rendall, Steven, University of Notre Dame Press, Notre Dame.

Human Rights Watch (1992) Israeli interrogation methods under fire after death of detained Palestinian, *Human Rights Watch* 4: available at www.hrw.org/reports/1992/israel/.

Ignatieff, Michael (2004) *The Lesser Evil: Political Ethics in an Age of Terror*, Princeton University Press, Princeton.

Ignatieff, Michael (2005) Moral prohibition at a price, in Roth, K. and Worden, M. (eds.) (2005), 18–27.

Independent (2006) Beckett admits Guantanamo Bay camp should be shut down, 13 October: available at www.news.independent.co.uk/uk/politics/article/1868066.ece.

Israeli Supreme Court (1999) Judgement on the interrogation methods applied by the GSS: available at www.derechos.org/human-rights/mena/doc/torture.html.

Jackson, Richard (2005a) The discursive construction of torture in the war on terrorism: narratives of danger and evil, paper delivered to a conference on the Barbarization of Warfare, University of Wolverhampton, 27–28 June: published in Kassimeris, G. (ed.) (2006), 141–170.

Jackson, Richard (2005b) *Writing the War on Terrorism: Language, Politics and Counter-terrorism*, Manchester University Press, Manchester.

Jehl, Douglas (2005) Questions are left by CIA chief on the use of torture, *New York Times*, 18 March, Section A, 1, col. 5.

Jones, Gary (1980) On the permissibility of torture, *Journal of Medical Ethics*, 6, 11–15.

Kadish, Sanford (1989) Torture, the state and the individual, *Israel Law Review*, 23, 345–356.

Kassimeris, G. (ed.) (2006) *Warrior's Dishonour: Barbarity, Morality and Torture in Modern Warfare*, Ashgate, Aldershot.

Kertész, Istvan (2006) *Fateless*, Vintage, London.

Klein, Naomi (2005) The true purpose of torture, *Guardian*, 14 May, 3: available at www.guardian.co.uk/comment/story/0,,1483801,00.html.

Kooijmans, Pieter (1995) Torturers and their masters, in Crelinsten, R. and Schmid, A. (eds.) (1995), 13–18.

Kreimer, Seth (2003) Too close to the rack and screw, *University of Pennsylvania Journal of Constitutional Law*, 6, 278–325.

Kremnitzer, Mordecai and Segev, Re'em (2000) The legality of interrogational torture: a question of proper authorization or a substantive moral issue?, *Israel Law Review*, 34, 509–559.

Langbein, John (1977) *Torture and the Law of Proof: Europe and England in the Ancien Régime*, Chicago University Press, Chicago.

Langbein, John (2004) The legal history of torture, in Levinson, S. (ed.) (2004), 93–104.

Langguth, A. L. (1978) *Hidden Terrors: The Truth about US Police Operations in Latin America*, Pantheon, New York.

Le Guin, Ursula (2000) The ones who walk away from Omelas, in *The Wind's Twelve Quarters*, Gollancz, London.

Levin, Michael (1982) The case for torture, *Newsweek*, 7 June, 13: available at www.people.brandeis.edu/~teuber/torture.html.

Levinson, Sanford (2003) The debate on torture, *Dissent*, Summer, unpaginated: available at www.dissentmagazine.org/article/?article=490.

Levinson, Sanford (2004) Contemplating torture: an introduction, in Levinson, S. (ed.) (2004), 23–43.

Levinson, Sanford (ed.) (2004) *Torture: A Collection*, Oxford University Press, Oxford.

Lippman, Matthew (1979) The protection of universal human rights: the problem of torture, *Universal Human Rights*, 1, 25–55.

Luban, David (2005) Liberalism, torture, and the ticking bomb, *Virginia Law Review*, 91, 1425–1461.

Lukes, Steven (2006) Liberal democratic torture, *British Journal of Political Science*, 36, 1–16.

Machan, Tibor (1991) Exploring extreme violence (torture), *Journal of Social Philosophy*, 19, 92–97.

May, Larry (2005) Torturing detainees during interrogation, *International Journal of Applied Philosophy*, 19, 193–208.

Miller, Seamus (2005) Is torture ever morally justified?, *International Journal of Applied Philosophy*, 19, 179–192.

Moore, Michael (1989) Torture and the balance of evils, *Israel Law Review*, 23, 280–344.

Morgan, Rod (2000) The utilitarian justification of torture: denial, desert and disinformation, *Punishment and Society*, 2, 181–196.

Pachecco, Allegra (1999) *The Case Against Torture in Israel: A Compilation of Petitions, Briefs and Other Documents Submitted to the Israeli High Court of Justice*, Public Committee Against Torture in Israel, Jerusalem: available at www.stoptorture.org.il/eng/publications.asp?menu=7&submenu=2.

Parry, John (2004) Escalation and necessity: defining torture at home and abroad, in Levinson, S. (ed.) (2004), 145–164.

Parry, John (2005) The shape of modern torture: extraordinary rendition and ghost detainees, *Melbourne Journal of International Law*, 6, 516–533.

Parry, John and White, Welsh (2002) Interrogating suspected terrorists: should torture be an option?, *University of Pittsburgh Law Review*, 63, 743–766.

Paskins, Barrie (1976) What's wrong with torture?, *British Journal of International Studies*, 2, 138–148.

Paskins, Barrie (1978) Reply [to Twining], *Proceedings of the Aristotelian Society (Supplement)*, 52, 168–178.

Peters, Edward (1999) *Torture*, University of Pennsylvania Press, Philadelphia, expanded edition.

Plaxton, Michael (2005) Torture warrants, hypocrisy and supererogation: justifying bright-line rules as if consequences mattered, paper presented at the conference on the Barbarization of Warfare, University of Wolverhampton, 27–28 June: published in Kassimeris, G. (ed.) (2006), 205–222.

Pokempner, D. (2005) Command responsibility for torture, in Roth, K. and Worden, M. (eds.) (2005), 158–172.

Pollard, Matt (2005) The absolute and comprehensive prohibition of torture and other cruel, inhuman or degrading treatment or punishment, Swedish Forum on Human Rights, Stockholm, 16–17 November: available at www.apt.ch/un/TortureProhibition_SFHR.pdf.

Posner, Richard (2004) Torture, terrorism, and interrogation, in Levinson, S. (ed.) (2004), 291–298.

Press, Eyal (2003) Tortured logic: thumbscrewing international law, *Amnesty Magazine*, summer, 2: available at www.amnestyusa.org/magazine/tortured/html.

Priest, Dana and Gellman, Barton (2002) US decries abuse but defends interrogations, *Washington Post*, 26 December, A01.

Quinton, Anthony (1971) Views, *The Listener*, 2 December, 757–758.

Roach, Kent (2003) *September 11: Consequences for Canada*, McGill-Queen's University Press, Montreal/Kingston.

Robin, Corey (2005) Protocols of machismo, *London Review of Books*, 19, 11–14.

Rose, David (2004) *Guantanamo: America's War on Human Rights*, Faber and Faber, London.

Roth, Kenneth (2005) Justifying torture, in Roth, K. and Worden, M. (eds.) (2005), 184–202.

Roth, Ken and Worden, Minky (eds.) (2005) *Torture*, New Press and Human Rights Watch, New York.

Scarry, Elaine (1985) *The Body In Pain*, Oxford University Press, New York.

Scarry, Elaine (2004) Five errors in the reasoning of Alan Dershowitz, in Levinson, S. (ed.) (2004), 281–299.

Scheppele, Kim Lane (2005) Hypothetical torture in the "war on terrorism", *Journal of National Security Law and Policy*, 1, 285–340.

Schroeder, Doris (2006) A child's life or a "little bit of torture"? State-sanctioned violence and dignity, *Cambridge Quarterly of Healthcare Ethics*, 15, 188–201.

Sheleff, Leon (1987) *Ultimate Penalties: Capital Punishment, Life Imprisonment, Physical Torture*, Ohio State University Press, Columbus.

Sheleff, Leon (2002) The necessity of defence of the truth: on the torturous deliberations about the use of torture, *Bar Ilan Law Studies*, 17, 485–488.

Shue, Henry (1978) Torture, *Philosophy and Public Affairs*, 7, 124–143. Reprinted in Levinson, S. (ed.) (2004), 47–60.

Solomon, Alisa (2001) The case against torture, *Village Voice*, November 28–December 4, 2: available at www.villagevoice.com/news/0148,fsolomon,30292,1.html.

Strauss, Marcy (2004) Torture, *New York Law School Law Review*, 48, 201–274.

Sussman, Donald (2005) What's wrong with torture?, *Philosophy and Public Affairs*, 33, 1–33.

Thomson, Judith Jarvis (1985) The trolley problem, *Yale Law Journal*, 94, 1395–1415.

Times Higher Education Supplement (2005) Make torture legal, say law academics, *THES*, 27 May, 14.

Tindale, Christopher (1996) The logic of torture, *Social Theory and Practice*, 22, 349–374.

Tindale, Christopher (2005) Tragic choices: reaffirming absolutes in the torture debate, *International Journal of Applied Philosophy*, 19, 209–222.

Trigg, Roger (2004) *Morality Matters*, Blackwell, Oxford.

Twining, W. (1978) Torture and philosophy, *Proceedings of the Aristotelian Society*, 52 (Supplement), 143–168.

Twining, W. L. and Twining, P. E. (1973) Bentham on torture, *Northern Ireland Legal Quarterly*, 24, 307–356.

United Nations Convention Against Torture (1984) Available at www.un.org/documents/ga/res/39/a39r046.htm.

Vidal-Naquet, Pierre (1963) *Torture: Cancer of Democracy: France and Algeria 1954–62*, Penguin, Harmondsworth.

Wagner, Markus (2003) The justification of torture. Some remarks on Alan M. Dershowitz's *Why Terrorism Works*, 4 *German Law Journal* 5, 1 May, 1–6: available at www.germanlawjournal.com/article.php?id=274.

Waldron, Jeremy (2005) Torture and positive law: jurisprudence for the White House, *Columbia Law Review*, 105, 1681–1750.

Walzer, Michael (1973) Political action: the problem of dirty hands, *Philosophy and Public Affairs*, 2, 160–180. Reprinted in Levinson, S. (ed.) (2004), 61–75.

Walzer, Michael (2003) Interview, *Imprints* 7, 4: available at www.eis.bris.ac.uk/~plcdib/imprints/michaelwalzerinterview.html.

Wiesel, Elie (1981) *Night*, Penguin, Harmondsworth.

Zamir, Itzhak (1989) Human rights and national security, *Israel Law Review*, 23, 375–406.

Ziv, Hadas (undated) Physicians and torture – the case of Israel, *Physicians for Human Rights – Israel*: available at www.hdip.org/Health&the-uprising-1.htm.

Žižek, Slavoj (2002) *Welcome to the Desert of the Real*, Verso, London.

Žižek, Slavoj (2006) The depraved heroes of 24 are the Himmlers of Hollywood, *Guardian*, 10 January, 27.

Index

and corruption of US culture   69
effectiveness condition   16,
    24–6, 29, 30, 33, 35, 37
fantasy construct   ix, 8–9, 16,
    17–18, 22, 31, 33–4, 38, 39, 40,
    75, 86
knowledge condition   31–5
and the "new realism"   11
probability   36–7, 58
time condition   16, 27–8, 30–1,
    33, 35, 38
uncritical acceptance of   16, 22
and the war on terror   85
see also thought-experiments
time condition   16, 27–8, 30–1, 33,
    35, 38
Tindale, Christopher   5, 10, 22–3,
    37, 76
torture   see abolition of torture;
    borderline cases of torture;
    "breaking" the tortured
    person; death, torture and;
    defining torture; degrees of
    torture; describing torture;
    drugs, torture and; experience
    of torture; habit-forming
    aspect of torture;
    institutionalization of torture;
    "intelligent torture";
    interrogational torture;
    intimidatory torture; "just in
    case" torture; justification of
    torture; legalization of torture;
    legislative standards for
    torture; lethal torture; limits to
    torture; "maximalist" torture;
    medical complicity in torture;
    moral duty to torture; "new
    realism" about torture; non-
    interrogational torture;
    normalization of torture; off-
    the-book system of torture;

pre-emptive use of torture;
    professional torturers;
    professionalization of torture;
    prohibition against torture;
    quasi-legal status of torture;
    rendition; resistance to torture;
    responsibility for torture,
    shifting; routinization of
    torture; spread of torture;
    survivors of torture; third
    party, torture of; torture
    warrants
"torture lite"   82–3
torture warrants   viii, 5, 7, 15, 16,
    23, 27–8, 35, 53, 61, 83, 84
    administrative issues   16, 30, 54,
    64
    issuing   6, 30, 34, 36, 65
    scope of   58
    threshold of torture, setting   36
    withholding, problems of   54
train driver scenario   14, 21, 22, 23,
    24, 48, 49, 52, 72
Turkey   68
Twining, W. L. and P. E.   32–3, 54–5

United Kingdom
    interrogational practices in
    Northern Ireland   25, 62
    London bombings (July 2005)   8,
    67
    Prevention of Terrorism Act
    2005   54
United Nations Convention Against
    Torture   5
United States
    military interrogation   24
    Patriot Act 2001   54
    retreat from moral high
    ground   63
    underwriting of torture   2, 63
    see also war on terror